Winners Never Quit

Winners Never Quit

Marguerite Rogers Howie:
African American Woman Sociologist

Gordon D. Morgan

New Academia Publishing, LLC
Washington, DC

New Academia Publishing, 2006

Printed in the United States of America

Library of Congress Control Number: 2006928664
ISBN 0-9777908-9-4 paperback (alk. paper)

New Academia Publishing, LLC
P.O. Box 27420 - Washingotn, DC 20038-7420
www.newacademia.com - info@newacademia.com

Contents

Preface

I have long been interested in sociology as biography and autobiography. Works have been published entitled *Lawrence A. Davis: Arkansas Educator* (New York; Associated Faculty Press, 1985), *Ida Rowland Bellegarde: Master Teacher/Scholar* (New York: McGraw-Hill, Inc., 1992), and *Tilman C. Cothran: Second Generation Sociologist* (Bristol, IN: Wyndham Hall Press, 1994).

I promised Marguerite Rogers Howie that I would do this work on her life in the Association of Social and Behavioral Sciences. It was some time after that communication with her eased and I learned that she had passed. It must have been in 1997 or 1998. Not only is this a comment on her work as a sociologist, but also is an installment of respect on the promise I made to her. She was a friend as well as a colleague.

Gordon D. Morgan, University Professor, University of Arkansas, Fayetteville 2005

Introduction

A whole generation of black social scientists has been lost. The first generation, represented by such scholars in sociology as E.F. Frazier, W.E.B. Du Bois, Carter G. Woodson, Charles S. Johnson, Allison Davis, Oliver C. Cox, St. Clair Drake, Horace Cayton, Ira de Reid, Mozell Hill, and Charles Gomillion, overshadowed those who came afterwards. These men worked to define and redefine the field of race relations. They were pioneers in the sense that they were not hesitant about placing their thought into the public domain to be discussed, even criticized, by those within and outside of black society. By studying in the mainstream universities, they emerged filled up with a desire to apply the knowledge gained to their own environments. They thought that change would follow in the wake of the accumulation of knowledge. For them knowledge would make them, and the rest of society, free. That was the driving religion of men like Charles S. Johnson, who were so devoted to the accumulation of facts with which there could be little argument.

A mythology grew up around these men and their work, taken collectively. Reference to them could easily become evidence that one had not completely ignored black scholarship. Once a ritual bowing had been made to them, their work was ignored and movement continued toward emphasis on the work of more current members of the mainstream. The conflict, for instance, between W.E.B. Du Bois and Booker T. Washington, though continuing from around the 1890s through Washington's death in 1915, classic as it was, ignored that there were others involved in the issue of defining black social change.[1] Charles S. Johnson's work on plantations was no doubt relevant for the times but could not stand as a permanent statement of the black condition in later years. Nor could Allison Davis's work with John Dollard and the Gardners forever define and explain Southern black life and the psychology it generated. The life of the urban ghetto could no longer be accurately described by the work of St. Clair Drake and Horace Cayton in their 1944 study entitled *Black Metropolis*.

Mainstream social science seemed intent on fixing, if not exclusively, then extensively, upon the work of these pioneers who deserved all the credit they justly received. Although they were referred to relatively often, they were not taken seriously to fit into any theoretical schemas to the extent that they were more than cursorily discussed. Almost no black women scholars were considered during this time. What few there were found it more expedient to work in the field of poetry, drama, and literature.[2]

But black society did not remain the same, as no society does. The teachings of these scholars must be seen within the context which then defined the discipline of sociology. As difficult as it was to break, as opprobrious as was the situation, the fact remained that America was badly divided racially. That fact was the principal generator of black sociological scholarship. Any social science presented for public reading had to take that reality into consideration. The very language used by mainstream sociology was supportive of that reality. The concept "caste" seems to have driven much of that sociology. Black scholars were bound to write within the constraints of that concept as well, with a few exceptions, such as O. C. Cox, although almost none of the early scholars showed evidence of internalizing that idea. Other members of the first generation had not been fortunate enough to get their work published and so were not given much credit for arguing against the caste concept. William Leo Hansberry, at Howard University, though not in sociology, was not awarded the Ph.D. degree at Harvard, allegedly for failure to adhere to mainstream thought that he showed to be flawed. Hansberry[3] had claimed for long years, that Ethiopia deserved much larger recognition than it was receiving as a candidate for location of the origin of civilization. George G. M. James, of British Guyana, had been arguing since the early 1930s that the Egyptians, really Africans, who would now be thought of as Subsaharan, were the ones from whom the Greeks gained their knowledge of science and mathematics.[4]

These first generation scholars conducted their studies in environments that were not conducive to the spread of critical black scholarship. The black schools in which most of them taught felt it dangerous politically to exhibit too high a degree of scholarship, especially that which did not support the status quo. They sensed the dangers in which they worked, but some of them persevered. Their main function, though, was to teach the next generation, and to prepare them to continue their work toward correction of the social system. For them teaching the next generation was absolutely essential if the struggle was to be continued.

The low visibility environments in which they worked proved to be advantageous and at the same time limiting. On the limiting side, they were denied well-deserved recognition in the discipline mainstream. In the advantage category must be the freedom they experienced to do practically whatever they wanted, to say whatever they pleased, so long as it was not published. They could literally indoctrinate the students with all they knew, even to a critical review and questioning of the social structure. The larger system would not know what they were doing and so no one would get hurt. Knowledge accumulated within the heads of the students, as it had been done in Africa and other colonial situations for hundreds of years.

Knowledge not published in no way suggests it did not exist. With a few exceptions, black scholars became something like griots, people to whom their people could turn for answers to their problems. The idea of the African American griot is not far fetched. In practically every community there are a few people who have more extensive knowledge of the history of the community than others. Oftentimes they are the oldest people.[5] This knowledge was not generally shared with mainstream society. The knowledge that was being accumulated in these environments was critical to the continued operation of those communities. The adjustment that black communities made to the mainstream was due largely to the application of knowledge that flowed from the black centers of knowledge, represented largely by teachers at those schools. Those with knowledge led relatively insulated lives that, to the outside appeared mysterious. It was not always the ingenuity of the black people that enabled their survival and relative prosperity during the days of separation. The skills had to be gained somewhere. It was in the schools that the knowledge base was acquired to practice medicine, even through midwifery), to repair vehicles, to establish newspapers, to draw house plans, and to carry out a thousand other activities within the community, activities that could not have been easily learned in the majority communities. Most of this knowledge was not formally organized, but it existed and was used.

Perhaps the greatest contribution of the black schools was their continuing preparation of black students for life in the mainstream. Their change from rough plantation and rural living toward that expected in the mainstream required much attention. This was a more important task than publishing books and papers that would earn one little recognition, if any, among mainstream scholars.

It was the charge of the first generation to pass this knowledge and orientation down to the second. It was well into the 1950s before it became safe enough in the institutions to conduct studies that were critical of the mainstream. By this time, the Civil Rights Movement was becoming extremely problematic. In Southern society, where the black colleges were located, there were greater recalcitrance and objection to change. The schools found themselves under threat of defunding. Scholarship of a critical nature slipped into the background and black scholars were shunted from one school to another, but seldom to mainstream ones. Men like Charles G. Gomillion,[6] at Tuskegee, were expected to be quiet. At Howard, E.F. Frazier turned his frustration onto black society in a bitter criticism of it in his *Black Bourgeoisie* (1957). After his 1948 critique of capitalism, and exposure of the mistakes of Gunnar Myrdal, O.C. Cox[7] left Tuskegee and headed for Lincoln University, where he could function better in the Border South-Midwestern state of Missouri where political and ethnic sensitivities were not as great as in the Deep South.

Some members of the second generation were not sufficiently steeled in the problems of southern social science teaching that they were losing their reticence or hesitancy to write. For some time they continued to examine aspects of black society. Hylan Lewis published *Blackways of Kent* (1955). It adhered closely to the Chicago School tradition with an emphasis on the internal dynamics of black social status. Tilman C. Cothran, arguably one of the most promising of the second generation sociologists, decided to concentrate his attention for a few more years on the preparation of future black scholars who would be freer to take up the cudgels against the forces opposing social change.[8] For the most part, second generation scholars continued to define their roles as Cothran had done and did not themselves produce impressive works, although their promise was great.

Many of those scholars are not noted in the footnotes to scholarly books and papers, and the assumption may be incorrectly drawn that they were not active in sociological work. Like many achievements, the works of these scholars were good for their time, but they were not preserved. The standards of academic work were changing, and had changed, while these persons were in mid-careers. When they began, academic work meant work with students, processing them toward citizenship, but not necessarily into a separate environment. When it became clear that a substantial number of these students, as adult citizens, would live outside the black community, the students were better prepared for the changes than their instructors, many of whom were not required to change. Where the standard was shifted to scholarly productivity, and they had not accepted that as their emphasis, it was difficult for them to be noted, except in the folklore of the students who had them as teachers. At nearly every black college, and probably at others in the country, there were personalities on the campus who were noted for their work, whether that work was scholarly or inspirational. Their lives merged with the ambience of their campuses; their satisfaction was in how well their students did, not how well they themselves did. They, like black public teachers, toiled in atmospheres yet defined by hostility toward the advancement of black people. There were few other choices than the schools to provide for the movement of thousands of black youth into roles of respectability.

This work on Marguerite Rogers Howie, herself a second generation sociologist, is intended to inquire into the processes in which that generation worked, how they adjusted, and to estimate their influence upon their school environments. Gaps in history need to be filled. Understanding of social life needs to be advanced. Society is made up of individuals whose lives are mirrors of its operation for particular times. By studying the life and work of a scholar such as Marguerite Howie, insights may be gained into how society worked at the intersections of class, race, and gender.

If the name of Marguerite Rogers Howie is unknown to legions of scholars, there are reasons for its not being so. She toiled in virtual isolation from mainstream scholarship, a condition not uncommon for many scholars of minority status.

The author wishes to thank the Association of Social and Behavioral Scientists for its support of this effort in appreciation of Professor Howie's work. It was hoped that it could stand as a volume of the *Journal of the Association of Social and Behavioral Sciences*. All the readers of this work who made valuable suggestions, particularly Delores Aldridge, Steven K. Worden, Talmadge Anderson and Frank Harold Wilson, are thanked generously. My assistant of the time Narraca Stubblefield is also to be thanked for interest in and deep devotion to the completion of this project. Izola Preston has continued to encourage me for many years and I thank her kindly for her consideration and help in both conceptualization and research relevant to this project. For all of its shortcomings the author alone is responsible.

It is more important than ever that we write the biographies of those people who struggled in the trenches, at the barricades, trying to bring about positive social change. The case of Marguerite Rogers Howie, born in 1919, is more illustrative than thought. The problem is that the people, even her friends, hailed her at the Association meetings, talked of her direct connection to W.E.B. Du Bois, but failed to discuss the possibility of the publication of her biography as either a journal article or as an occasional paper by the Association.

It was very strange how these people threw Marguerite Howie to the wind, with no real recognition of her tireless work for the Association. It was probably not the members closest to Marguerite Howie's generation that rejected her, but those that were much younger and trying to use the Association journal to further their own professional advancement. Former officers monopolized issues of the journal and showed little interest in the work on Howie, despite the fact that by then she had two strokes and was unable to plead her case. She would inevitably drift further into the background.

I cannot make Marguerite Howie's name a household word in black sociological scholarship. I can only try to see that the same fate does not befall her as met other scholars who tried to make a difference. Perhaps the younger scholars, themselves very insecure in their quests for tenure, do not see memorializing ordinary people, even teachers at any level of teaching, as a good use of resources. Nor could the failure to endorse Howie for publication mean a great saving to the Association. The Association *Journal* is several years behind. Not enough material is coming forward to fill up those issues while printing prices are rising. The few issues that are coming out are usually combined and practically monopolized by a few individuals closely situated in positions of power in the Association.

I guess I could have made an issue over the Howie matter, but I did not. To do so would make no point other than to further strain the relationships between the youthful and more senior members of the Association. It is now clear that the only thing the young members want from the older ones is their money. Whatever they do for seniors seems more an attempt to get them to contribute money. They may lionize them for a few moments, but is it all phony? It seems to be. The Association membership stabilizes around a group that is itself unstable. Standing in the Association changes because, for some years, there has not been a forceful Executive Secretary. In the past, that official literally ran the Association because the Executive Secretary knew more about the organization than anyone else, including the personalities in it. That officer kept up with those matters that affected the Association. He or she did not have all that much opposition and was expected to make the right decisions for the Association. Marguerite Howie served as Association Executive Secretary for several years. During that time she continued to exercise a positive influence.

When Howie retired from her school, her status, even in the Association changed, although it took several years for that change to be noted. She had no institutional role, or at least not one that was greatly respected. She found it difficult to carry the day in the Association. Many of the younger scholars did not know her and, more importantly, they were not very interested in what she was saying. During her last years in the Association, she had to become much more combative in order to be heard.

Background to the Project

During the annual meetings of the Association of Social and Behavioral Scientists at Tallahassee, Florida, March 8-12, 1995, there were occasions for meeting old friends who had not been seen for the last year and often for many years. Between sessions some repaired to rooms where visiting continued. James Conyers[9] invited the author and Marguerite Howie[10] to visit for a minute in his room. There discussion turned to talk about past Association members and their work. The author told Conyers and Professor Howie about a book that was scheduled for release in 1995 about the late Tilman C. Cothran, a scholar who had a big influence on the production of black social scientists. Cothran had labored long at Arkansas Agricultural, Mechanical and Normal College (now the University of Arkansas at Pine Bluff), later at Atlanta University, where he was joined in sociology by Conyers, and still later at Western Michigan University, Kalamazoo, where he served as associate dean of the College of Arts and Sciences.[11] Much discussion ensued about the work and mannerisms of Professor Cothran and how various students and other constituents saw him.

The author took the position that, even though individuals had different faces, and carried out different duties, they generally had group development in mind and wanted to be remembered for those activities. Recognizing the contributions of these hardworking members has been too often overlooked. It was noted that perhaps younger scholars who have been touched by some of these figures would have the energy to bring attention to them through the writing of booklength manuscripts on them. A few of the more notable scholars have been written about because of their outstanding theoretical or disputational contributions to the discipline. Horace Cayton and St. Clair Drake are well known for their *Black Metropolis* (1944). Allison Davis wrote with Burleigh and Mary Gardner and occasionally with John Dollard in studies of the caste systems of the South. Charles S. Johnson's studies of sharecroppers gained some notoriety before the 1950s, as did the family and social class studies of E. Franklin Frazier. Many other scholars carried out studies which were quite highly recognized by social scientists. Mozell Hill became quite well known as an academic sociologist through his studies of small towns of the Border and Deep South states. John Hope Franklin's *From Slavery to Freedom* has gone through some seven editions to become practically the bible of black history. Du Bois has no doubt been a most interesting topic. More has been written about him, his work, and opinions, than any other black scholar. So overwhelming is the reputation of Du Bois that when black social scientists are mentioned, his name almost automatically comes to attention.

Although there was not much emphasis, relatively speaking, upon the contributions of black scholars, female scholars were very hard to find, although they were active. Adelaide M Cromwell[12] studied the class structure of black Boston and Carolyn Bond Day[13] studied the social structures of mixed race people. Ida Rowland Bellegarde had been studying and writing since the late 1930s and found the best format for her work to be in the form of poems. Her *Lisping Leaves*[14] gained notable reviews. These studies were more likely to come to the attention of students but none of them reached a wide readership. Since most of these studies were during the period of rank separation of the races, they coincided with the period in which women had the fewest opportunities for gaining recognition in academe, even within the black schools.

Probably the best test of whether a black social scientist or other scholar or leader has had any influence on either students or a wider constituency is whether that person has had a book written on his or her life. Occasionally, the scholars pen their own biographies but these very seldom find their way into print for consumption by a wider audience. During the lifetimes of some individuals they are taken on over, lionized, but soon thereafter, they are forgotten and nobody remembers their names. Not all of the scholars have been noted for their academic contributions. Others have taken other tacks and have worked more closely with students in preparing them for continued study and achievement in their chosen fields.

1
Toiling in the Trenches

Marguerite Rogers Howie

I began attending the meetings of the Association of Social and Behavioral Scientists in 1966. That year I saw a smallish, attractive, activist woman, then in early middle age, not all that much older than myself, who was very visible in the affairs of the association. She was what we called feisty because she was so enthusiastic about what she advocated. It was very clear then that Marguerite Howie was destined for leadership in the association because she was so committed. Although there were a few majority members in the association, it was difficult to place Marguerite Howie. She looked like a majority member, but behaved like someone who had been closely connected with the African American group. She was extremely friendly and seemed to know most of the members in the association on a first name basis. It was several years before I learned that she was teaching at South Carolina State University.

As the years passed Marguerite Howie assumed more and more leadership showing the same kind of competitiveness and commitment that she exhibited evidently from the earliest of her attendance at the association meetings. What was most noticeable was that Marguerite Howie began early to try to transfer her enthusiasm for the study of black society first, and then the larger society, to the younger students and faculty members. She had been highly influenced by the work of W.E.B. Du Bois which became quite apparent when she received the Association's Du Bois Award in 1984 in Nashville, Tennessee. She helped encourage the organization leadership to hold the Du Bois Luncheon at Fisk University where Du Bois was a student and where he later taught. Aside from the Fisk Jubilee Singers, Du Bois is undoubtedly the most widely known graduate of the institution. Howie cited Du Bois for other than his academic and activist work. She took as her theme Du Bois' suggestion that people who were interested in change needed to "get fired up and stay fired up."[1] Professor Howie's address was a very moving one which rechallenged the group to do all each individual could in his or her environment to bring about positive change. The leaders in so many of the communities were in the educational field, where they worked for boards which were often hostile toward black improvement even though their memberships might be considered as liberal. Howie reminded the group that Du Bois was not intimidated by those people who were most opposed to black improvement. Much of this work would be thankless for there would not be the means to bring wide attention to it. Persons in small places would be practically unrecognized although the people they served were in conditions more desperate than those in the larger cities which had greater access to the media. Workers in the outlying provinces were more vulnerable to reprisals and dismissal by autocratic and vindictive overseers than those in the larger places where the media were more aggressive and less constrained. It was the encouragement given by such persons as Marguerite Howie that has been most useful to those young people at work in the smaller places, in the places of quite limited recognition.

Howie was very aware of the vulnerabilities which black faculty members faced in their schools. The folklore was that if they got out of line the benefits to the school would fail to come. In South Carolina where the ratio of blacks to whites had always been high, during and after slavery, the hostility of the majority group leaders toward blacks was sharp. Perhaps most critical was the failure of the state to open channels of education for the blacks while not allowing them to attend the majority institutions in any significant numbers. The alternative was to turn the field of minority education over to church related institutions. Benedict, Vorhees, Claflin, St. Paul's, and a few other institutions sought to fill the void created by the poor state attitude toward the advancement of black higher education. The state worked to assure that the black college remained an uninviting place for those to work who had academic orientations. Charles U. Smith reported in 1968 that:

> the predominantly Negro college developed, survived and exists
> to the present day in largely a social psychological environment
> of isolation, apathy, paternalism, and stigma. In the early years of
> the establishment of the Negro college in the later Reconstruction
> and early post-Reconstruction years, such an institution possibly

could not have survived without virtually completely isolating itself from the dominant white society. The reascendancy of the white aristocracy; the declarations of unconstitutionality of the civil rights legislation of the reconstruction years, plus the enforcement of the "black codes" separated the institutional world of the Negro almost totally from that of the whites.

Therefore, the Negro college became a relatively self-contained community in itself with its own food services, laundry and cleaning services, entertainment activities and on-campus concerns, unofficially and officially discouraging the participation of students and faculty in community activities.[2]

When Marguerite Howie's generation of social scientists were ready to begin their practice and studies, there was no great hue and cry anywhere in the country for social science research. The problems were not viewed as susceptible to correction by the efforts of the most outstanding minds from the institutions of knowledge. There was very little financial or social incentive to undertake this research. And even if interesting findings were delivered they were likely to be ignored by those in policy-making positions. There was little market for this research in any of the communities to which the findings related.

The language was often esoteric, technical, and academically strained. Studies were not very likely to find their way into the public domain. Nor were studies discussed much beyond the walls of academe. Overall the situation was discouraging of the conduct of research by most of the scholars at the schools of small influence. After a scholar had completed a thesis or dissertation other claims were made on his or her time and energies. It was only in the late 1950s or early 1960s that a well-qualified black scholar had to worry about tenure. Until that time almost all who were minimally qualified and wanted it could receive tenure and enticement to settle into a life of limited academic productivity.

On the campuses the dominant personality was the president who was accused of brooking no challenge to his dominance by any of his faculty members. This, of course, was more stereotype than truth for in very few cases did a black scholar arise to challenge the president for local dominance. The most illustrative case is probably that of the dominant personalities of Booker T. Washington and George Washington Carver at Tuskegee. These men, both of international reputation, did not seem to be threats to each other. Both felt comfortable enough with their own accomplishments to not be threatened by the notoriety of the other. Indeed, it is said that Washington had suggested that Carver accept more of the speaking engagements for to do so would further the reputation of Tuskegee.

Probably it was only at Howard University, after the publicity of Washington and Carver at Tuskegee that noted faculty began to assert themselves. The fame of Carter G. Woodson in the field of Negro History in the 1920s could have become a problem for Mordecia Wyatt Johnson, the first black president of Howard. The scholars in the scientific fields such as Charles Drew and Ernest E. Just along with men such as Charles Evans Hughes and Thurgood Marshall in law served as challenges to the dominance of the Howard president who, arguably, laid claim to holding the most important position in Black America. The Howard University presidency made the incumbent the most visible black academic in the country. Social scientists of the later eminence of John Hope Franklin and E. Franklin Frazier had to tread carefully in the presence of the Howard University president lest it be thought that they were usurping some of his popularity.

It was substantially the same at other black colleges. At Southern University Felton G. Clark, who had inherited the position of president from his own father, was careful about allowing faculty members to become independent thinkers. They might upset the authorities responsible for the funding of the institution thereby damaging opportunities for education of hundreds or even thousands of youth badly needing it from Louisiana and other parts of the South and the country. Scholars like Blyden Jackson received much greater acclaim after leaving Southern. Jackson moved to the University of North Carolina at Chapel Hill where he became a distinguished member of the department of English. His books on the history of black literature became highly regarded offerings from the Louisiana State University Press.[3]

One of the reasons that black scholars in the early 1950s began to defect from the black colleges was because the scholastic norms were changing. Cleo Hearnton, professor of education at Arkansas AM&N College, Pine Bluff, bolted to the state university system of California where she stood a better chance of producing scholastic work. Ernest Works, upon receiving the Ph.D. in sociology at the University of Illinois in the early 1960s headed to the California system. James Conyers, who had worked at black colleges since the early 1950s, received the Ph.D. degree in 1962 and departed for Indiana State University, Terre Haute. Majority colleges seemed to have wanted the scholars at the time and made it more convenient for them to make academic contributions. John Hope Franklin began to be more productive when he left Howard, as did Edgar G. Epps upon leaving Tennessee State University to shortly find his way to the University of Chicago. Jackie Jackson was more productive at Duke University Medical School in the area of gerontology than she was at her previous posts at Southern University and later Howard. Wiliam Julius Wilson would have been a good candidate to return to Wilberforce where he received his baccalaureate degree. Upon receiving the Ph.D. he found greener pastures and opportunity for growth and productivity at University of Massachusetts, Amherst. From there he was tapped for the University of Chicago at which he became, arguably, America's most noted sociologist of the 1970s and 1980s, a role he retains at the present writing. In 1996 Wilson departed Chicago for Harvard with a well-established reputation. He was promoted to University Professor in 1998.

Norms changed more slowly at the black institutions. Presidents remained dominant figures, if not intimidating scholars, but certainly not widely encouraging their productivity. Although some black scholars continued to be productive at a few of the predominantly black colleges, the most did not engage in the forays. An article or two during their careers was the most that most could muster. Notable exceptions to that case is the work of Charles U. Smith, at Florida A&M University and Leon Prather at Tennessee State University. Almost all the first generation scholars were at work in black colleges where they gained some recognition for their work.[4]

By the late 1970s a substantial change had taken place with respect to black academic productivity with most of it coming from majority schools where black faculty members were becoming ensconced. Black students were enrolling at greater rates in the majority institutions, even in the junior and community colleges and fewer were opting for the training they could receive at the Historically Black Colleges and Universties. Less scholarly work was coming from those institutions as the issue of their role as teaching or more general purpose universities became vitriolic. An illustrative case of the conflict of purpose of these institutions was seen in the case of a black graduate scientist at North Carolina A&T State University. He received his terminal degree after military service and thought he could better serve the students at his institution by focusing on good teaching rather than research, grantsmanship, and publishing. He was threatened with dismissal by administrators wanting to convert A&T to a research institution. Allegations flew about that if the school itself were upgraded the administrators could claim higher salaries even though the evidence showed that undergraduate teaching suffers when the focus of the institution is on graduate studies and research.[5]

Marguerite Howie, a very longtime member of the Association of Social and Behavioral Scientists, was asked what students she knew, of the many she had taught, and evidently whose lives she influenced, would be candidates to write about her and the work she did. Professor Howie demurred for a moment and then offered that she did not know of any students who could or would perform that task. She was ambivalent about whether she had accomplished enough to merit that kind of effort in the first place.

James E. Conyers

Conyers and the author thought that Howie's long service to the Association of Social and Behavioral Scientists, literally from its very beginning, and the work she did through it, would qualify her for recognition. Even though Howie reluctantly agreed that she had been a long and willing worker, having graduated from college in 1939 when the Association was only four years old, and having known many of the earlier participants, she still wondered who would have the energy and enthusiasm to do the work. She thought she would not have such energy herself, having not at this point completed her own memoirs.

We finally convinced Howie that she was indeed a worthy subject, that much of the story of the Association could be told through her life. After further discussion, Conyers and Howie thought that the author would no doubt be the person most likely to see the project through to completion, if it were undertaken.

We concluded that meeting and the next day or so the author talked again with Professor Howie who agreed with the principle of a significant work about herself. She was willing to cooperate in any way she could. I talked with Professor Thessalonia Ford, of St. Louis Community College, and also a longtime member of the Association, about the possibility of a book about Ms. Howie. She thought it was a good idea and volunteered to help in whatever way she could. So did Ruth Dennis of Austin Peay State University. Professor Frances Staten, of Grambling State University, was interested in having her students undertake biographical works of people in their communities who deserve such attention. She was quite impressed by possibilities of the Marguerite Howie biography. Marguerite Howie was now one of the oldest members of the Association who had continuous attendance, responsibilities through office-holding, and recognition. She was closest to the founding of the Association and no doubt had the best feel for changes in it, as well as reasons for those changes.

When the author reached his home after the meetings, he found that the story of Marguerite Howie would not leave his mind, even though he had a number of other projects under way at the same time. For the next week the Howie book came to direct his thoughts. Perhaps his teaching suffered to some extent from this interest. Howie had worked so hard to promote the Association and had received its highest rewards and recognition and yet there was no student, or young faculty member who would take her on as a project. At least she could not think of any. Many of those who were relatively new to the Association, did not know of its history, or of the reputations of some members of the group. This was no doubt the case when Marguerite Howie began her participation some fifty years ago. Only later when her own maturity increased did she understand how sterling were their reputations.

After research began to get organized on the Howie biography, it was found that there had been no formal history of the Association, though there had been snippets, the most important being Robert Moran's historical sketch of the Association which appeared in the program of the annual meetings in Cleveland, Ohio, March 24-27, 1992. Moran had served as the archivist for the Association for some years and was no doubt in the best position to pen a history of the Association. His other duties and some health limitations prohibited his proceeding vigorously with that task.[6] The various issues of the *Journal of Social and Behavioral Sciences* did not contain, among the research and qualitative papers, any extensive history of the life of the Association. Occasionally, members who were distinguished social scientists were featured through articles on their lives and work. It now appeared that a biography on Marguerite Howie would at the same time be a history of the Association for the two were intimately intertwined.

But Marguerite Howie was not merely an Association woman. She was busy carrying out her own research and was independently recognized for her contributions. She served as Professor of Sociology at South Carolina State College and held an Endowed Chair as a Distinguished Professor in the School of Arts and Sciences. She received grants from Cooperative State Research Service/United States Department of Agriculture, the Russell Sage and Kellogg Foundations. A bibliography of her published work is printed in the Appendix.

There is a larger message in the writing of this book. The contention is that much may be learned about social life across time by focusing on individual life stories. Unlike questionnaire data, which generally provide a cameo or snapshot of a group and thereby dates it in time, the life story crosses time barriers, enabling understanding to be achieved while avoiding separation from the social context. The individual encounters many of the same problems of the group and thus becomes a sample of the group of which he or she is a part.[7]

Any individual is basically a study of the human condition for that person is ordinarily imbedded at some level in a social network, however loosely or tightly knit. The person cannot be understood without a close examination of those structures in which the person is imbedded. But it should not be thought that the person is only a passive factor for oftentimes the person alters or modifies the structure. Since each individual is unique, he or she may interact with or impact the structure in relatively unique ways. Marguerite Howie's own story will suggest how she affected and was affected by her first social unit, her family. She is not just a female who lived at a particular time and place. She represents, or could stand to represent, people of color, and especially women of color. She may serve as the focus of discussion of educated women and the problems they faced as well as the importance of age at various times as revealed in the group context. In her life will be found the tug of conflict between raising a family and adherence to longstanding community expectations, versus the growing social and economic independence of females. Insight into the influence of social class and the various desiderata of stratification will be seen in her life, as well as how the stratified groups related to each other in the daily lives of individuals inside the community and out. Her example illustrates strategies that different groups used to improve, first, the lives of individuals, and then how these strategies were applied to group improvement. In other words, the individual is in a variety of ways a microcosm of the group.

The focus of this study is on the sociological life of Marguerite Rogers Howie (born September 17, 1919, Raleigh, N.C., St. Agnes Hospital, 2 ½ lbs.), who became one of the early black women sociologists. Before her, other women had done sociological work but they have not been recognized. Generally, if they taught they were submerged in campus duties that so interfered with their scholarly efforts that many ceased any interest. Howie may have been one of the first black women scholars to attempt to work on a fulltime basis as a practicing (that is, researching) and teaching sociologist. General sociology books are only now beginning to recognize the work of Harriet Martineau, a contemporary of Auguste Comte and other founders of the discipline, probably only because of the influence of the Women's Liberation Movement of recent decades. For much of the 37 years that Marguerite Howie taught at South Carolina State College, later University, there were few opportunities to carry out respected sociological studies. Howie joined the faculty at South Carolina State College in the late 1950s. Evidently she was studying toward the doctoral degree for some time before joining the faculty there. In order to get a chance at hiring black faculty, it was not uncommon for presidents then to get their commitment when it appeared they would complete the degree. According to her vita sheet, Howie's first publication occurred in 1976, after a delay of nearly twenty years after her joining the faculty. For the first ten years of her tenure at South Carolina State Howie faced the usual problem of earlier academics, and that was a need for a doctoral degree for respectability on the campus. Movement in that direction was some evidence that the new hire had given up the quest. Between 1953 and 1963, Howie reached the dissertation stage as a doctoral candidate in Social Foundations, Sociology and Guidance. Just why she did not persist toward the degree is known only to herself. Perhaps she defined herself as somewhat mature for that time, although when she began her serious studies, she would have been about 35 years of age, about three years older than that at which regular sociology doctoral degrees were granted. The norm toward seeking higher degrees by persons of that maturity had not been established to the extent it has today.

The institution at that time was not focused as much on faculty contribution to scholarly work, but instead it was on the preparation of students for immediate placement in the world of work. While pressure was placed on the presidents to upgrade their faculties, the political situation did not force their upgrading. Few, if any, faculty members were fired for failing to obtain higher degrees although they may have been moved around if they had been at the institution for some years. If they were young and had received their terminal degrees, they may not have returned to the institution for more than a year or so because they could compete for better salaries by working at institutions that did not have black faculty members and that were in need of recruiting some. By waiting until the political waters became clearer, a scholar would more likely ride out any scares and hold on to his or her job without actually securing a terminal degree.

The black state college has always been a resource for the state in which it is located. Its faculty members are sought out wherever they are needed, especially in changing situations occasioned by the integration of schools, communities, and other facilities. Howie's studies on rural populations, aging, and other problematic categories led to her being asked to consult on the South Carolina Commission on Aging, Pre-retirement Council, 1974-79; the South Carolina Caucus on Black Aging, 1976-1986, the South Carolina Social Welfare Forum, Executive Board, 1978-1995, and the South Carolina Task Force on Aging, 1979-1986. She served on the Human Relations Forum, College of Charleston, March 1980.

Howie was also quite active on the South Carolina State College campus, serving as a member of the college faculty senate, 1969-1973, and 1977-1980. She was president of the Faculty Senate, 1978-1980.

The pattern exhibited in Howie's trajectory is probably quite typical of the women who entered academics at the time she did. Howie was more active than the majority of women academics of the time.

There were a number of campus societies that claimed the attention of faculty members such as Marguerite Howie. Early on she established herself as a promising scholar and was elected to Alpha Omicron Chapter of Alpha Kappa Mu Honor Society, at Shaw University, in 1938, the national black honorary society thought of as the equivalent of Phi Beta Kappa. When money and interest became available to recognize them, chairs were established at black schools. At South Carolina State College Marguerite Howie was named to the Distinguished Faculty Endowed Chair, which she held from 1982 through 1986. She was awarded emeritus status at the college in 1986.

The evidence is ample that Marguerite Howie was active in many phases of work at her college. Again, the intention in this work is concern with her work as a sociologist. It is necessary not to forget the circumstances in which she worked, along with many others in schools such as hers. There was bound to be a refocusing of efforts in schools like South Carolina State College, for the major output of students was into the public school teaching ranks. By the early 1970s, black graduates could not depend upon entry into the teaching field as they almost automatically did during the days before desegregation. Teachers in the colleges were unsure as to whether they were expected to be fulltime teachers or would they have research responsibilities? Some of those who could not adjust to the new requirements tried to hang on but had to move on, especially if they did not have tenure. For some of those who already had tenure, but who did not show effort toward research and writing, new positions on the campus, or in the organization awaited them. Teachers young enough to readjust were sent subtle messages that they needed to become academically productive for the black state colleges were being evaluated by the same criteria as the majority colleges.

2
Howie's Ambiguity

The Carolinas have been ambiguously located since the formation of the American colonies. The political and civil strife, allied with a lack of prosperity in the British Isles, mainly England, encouraged emigration to the American colonies. The Carolinas were founded in the late 1660s. Many of the English colonists had come from the West Indies, where they had engaged in the raising of plantation sugar and tobacco.[1] Others came directly from the British Isles where they were still ambivalent about whether they wanted a monarchial system of government and whether they wanted the institution of slavery. They could not agree economically, politically, or socially. Part of this territory belonged to the Scots-Irish tradition of individual freedom under Protestantism. Most of these immigrants were not opposed to the system of inherited status so reminiscent of the feudal system, nor did they endorse chattel slavery, although not all of them actively opposed it. As frontiersmen trying to upgrade to yeoman farmers, and later to businessmen, they were committed to carving out a way of life based on their individual initiative.

Ancient hostilities and animosities with the English over such matters as religion, the monarchy, and personal status, kept these groups from combining their resources to more thoroughly control the land.[2]

Topographically, the Carolinas were divided between hill and lowland. This natural division was soon associated with different ways of making a living. In the lowlands, where the land was more fertile, it was more valuable. If it were close to the water, the owners could reap benefits from both the sea and the land. They could engage in mixed strategies of acquisition. Owners in the lowlands were more committed to the accumulation of the symbols of status and wealth. Highlanders were in tenuous control of less productive land and were forced to raise crops that were suited to the topography. Where they raised the same crops as the lowlanders, the scale was much smaller. Family labor was more involved in the highlands than in the lowlands where gang and slave labor predominated. Some of the highlanders had help which were technically carried as slaves but, as in the other highland areas, it was most difficult to maintain the separation between the groups that existed in the lowlands. The homesteads and small farms were more widely separated and any slaves might have lived within the same household, or very close to it, as the regular householders lived. The issues of religion and slavery separated the Carolinas to the extent that they had to be divided into enclaves of Protestants who believed in slaveholding and those who did not. The issues of allegiance to the English crown were involved in this decision.

The tidewater Carolinas were the preserve of the English who attempted to establish large farms with the intention of reinstituting the essential features of the feudal system. Failing that they would recreate the system of status and hierarchy found in urban England. Their values were in that direction.

Although the hill people of the Carolinas usually had large families, they still needed labor. Some even took over care of young slaves and raised them along with their families, as a practical matter. These families did not have the funds or the facilities for complete separation. There was an inevitable mixing of the hill people and the slaves to the extent that within a few years there emerged whole groups and communities of highly mixed people in all the mountain provinces.[3] When these African Americans went to the cities, it was not uncommon for them to form communities separate from the regular black ones.

Before the Civil War, the offspring of island, French, and Catholic planters and businessmen, incorporated these highly mixed people into a social structure that favored them. The women were thought especially beautiful. After the Civil War, these octoroon, quadroon, and mulatto women came to be more desired among the freedmen and the members of the emerging black bourgeoisie.[4] The men did not fare so well and were seen, at least in informal reports, as persons of tragedy for they were marginalized through mixture to the extent they had no secure place in either majority or black society. Their status was rendered even more tenuous with the passage of Plessy v. Ferguson (1896) when the U. S. Supreme Court tried to define who was a Negro by use of the criterion that any degree of black ancestry defined one as a Negro.

Whether Marguerite Howie's studies of her own roots indicate it or not, it was well known by the time of her birth that there was a substantial grading by color in the Carolinas, as well as in other parts of America. In the tidewater areas where crops could be grown, especially rice, where gang and slave labor were needed, the social structure favored this arrangement. The backcountry people of North Carolina's hill country were known as "tarheels." Their independence extended to their free choice in association with whomever they pleased. They mixed with the slaves to the extent they pleased and considered it beyond the business of law or convention. Usually, by the time the law became involved, it was too late for children had been born and needed to be cared for.

The society had a hard choice of recognizing the then illegal arrangements practiced widely by the people, or caring for the children of mixed heritage. Since the means of charitable support were quite underdeveloped, there was little choice but to grumble about any unapproved relationships between people of different race. The focus then shifted to young people who sought to socialize across racial lines with severe penalties meted out to both the girl and the boy who violated social conventions disapproving of too close interracial fraternization, and of not much between classes. Howie was a product, however distant, of this interracial fraternization.

She was a very popular teacher at South Carolina State College when she began to work there in 1957; and she maintained that enthusiasm   for many years until her retirement in 1986. She was always very popular with members of her professional association and continued her popularity in her church and sorority relations.

From the time of the introduction of colonialism and slavery in the Latin provinces in the 1500s, and from 1621 when the first boatloads of slaves were brought to North America, attempts were made to reduce the cost of slavery such that more profits could accrue to the promoters of the institution. Many techniques were tried. One of the first was physical punishment through hard work and the breaking of the spirit of the bondmen. That proved too costly and labor had to be replaced with great frequency. There were too many runaways, too much rebellion, too much shirking of duties. Another way had to be found that was less costly and which promised greater results than the system based on suppression and punishment. This method involved the breaking in of the slaves so that they would adhere to the rules of work of the colonial masters. Their African culture was seen as valueless in the New World and was to be stamped out largely through their conversion to the Christian way of life. The hierarchies that had been emplaced in Europe were to be instituted in the New World colonies. Important in this building of hierarchies was color stratification. Generally, it was thought that those slaves genotypically and phenotypically closest to the Europeans would receive the most privileges. Basically, fair-skinned Africans, called mulattoes, quadroons, and octoroons, gained opportunities that the darker-skinned Africans did not have. A mulatto was the offspring of an African and a European; a quadroon has one black grandparent. An octoroon has one black great grandparent. These concepts were based on European racial reasoning that may not have had currency in other parts of the world. Nevertheless, they came to have much meaning in North American and Caribbean social structures.

When the U. S. Supreme Court tried to clarify who was of what racial category in Plessy v. Ferguson, a two tier system in the U. S. was created. That was a white-black dichotomy. All persons would fit in either of these two categories, although there were efforts of some groups, such as Orientals, to deny fitting into either of the categories. Generally, they were assigned to the black category and to those communities, if they could not manage separate communities. This ruling added to the mixing of the black group.

Native Americans found themselves facing the choice of being assigned to the reservation, if they did not want to be assigned to the black group. Many Orientals and Native Americans entered the black group, although some with the phenotypes and genotypes found security within the white group. In the mountains, where the groups were isolated, the mixing was relatively common. In time there was great color shading among the black group. Because they were separated from the majority group, to a great extent, there developed within black society an emphasis on color ranking.

By the time of the birth of Marguerite Howie in 1919, it was thought that some relationship existed between complexion and nearness to Anglo norms. Within black society, privileges, education, opportunities, and responsibilities were thought to be directly related to color. For a considerable while after slavery the newly opened higher schools catered very largely to the lighter-skinned blacks. In cities, and where they were located in large numbers, society life took place and was closely related to color. Students such as Marguerite Rogers experienced a little preferential treatment in their schools and were, no doubt, encouraged more than the others. Ordinarily, complexion alone was not enough to command privilege, but when color was combined with good family standing, it seemed to have greater payoff. Students familiar with the history of race relations in America, and with the social class system, will understand the place of color in the country. While color was thought advantageous to some, it was thought a liability in other cases. When it did not deliver the advantages some light-skinned people thought it should, they rebelled and tried to be the strongest fighters against the admission of color as a relevant social criterion.

In North Carolina, where Marguerite went to school, and at Shaw University, the relationship of color to social standing was perhaps as notable as at any other school in the country. The state itself had been a center of the "black bourgeoisie."[5] In the towns and cities, and especially around

Durham, and in the Triangle—Raleigh, Durham and Chapel Hill—as well as at Winston-Salem and Greensboro, this problem was especially keen. At the colleges the vast majority of campus beauties and queens picked by students were of light complexion, often with finely chiseled features, aristocratic in-steps, blue veins, and auburn hair. Although talent could not be denied when it was exhibited by persons without the credentials of color and family background, many of the clubs seemed to attract persons of lighter complexion.

On many campuses, and in various cities, the matter of color became an axis of conflict between lighter and darker-skinned blacks. As late as 1984, when the Association of Social and Behavioral Scientists met at Nashville, Tennessee, and scheduled a meeting and luncheon at Fisk University, a member went through Jubilee Hall and noticed the pictures on the wall of the historic building. She became angry and said that Fisk would not have allowed her to attend then; today she has no feeling for the school. She was dark and had a mild physical disability. Her hostility toward the mulattoes prominently displayed at Fisk made her wish the school would disappear. Similar reminders are found in various other schools today. Atlanta and Howard Universities have prominent displays of this type.

Marguerite Howe emerged at a time when the old aristocrats of black society were in decline, to a certain degree. They could no longer lay claim to the fact that they were closely related to the masters of the big houses. Massive changes in the economy of the U.S., war spending, the migration of blacks from South to North and the formation of newer pockets of wealth, poverty, and status, the greater availability of education, meant everything was changing. The old landmarks of status and recognition were not securely in place. Yet, South Carolina was one of the states where it was most difficult to overthrow the idea of the aristocracy of color. Willard Gatewood, writing about Asa H. Gordon, a black South Carolinian in the 1920s, notes:

> ...while a growing "group consciousness" was evident among blacks throughout his state, even in Charleston, there were still many many Negroes...who believe(d) in the principles of aristocracy...in the value of blue blood and in the privileges it presumably conferred.[6]

Color snobbishness remained a fact in black society, but there had to be recognition of achievement. Where old aristocrats, and those laying verbal if not practical claim to that status, thought that they could lighten their children and give them better advantages by marrying persons lighter than themselves, they found that in a cash economy, color credentials

did not have much payoff. A pretty light-skinned girl would be more inclined to marry a dark doctor than a light ne'er do well.

At Shaw University, in Raleigh, North Carolina, where Marguerite
Rogers received her bachelor's degree in 1939, an old black aristocracy had
been in formation for some time, but was losing its impact. Shaw had bid
to become an important school within the black pantheon of schools, joining Fisk, Atlanta University, Hampton, Bennett, Spelman, Howard, and a
few others as centers for the training of the black middle class. Shaw was
distinctive in that it at one time operated a black medical school (Leonard
Medical School), rivaling Meharry and Howard for that honor. It was almost natural that Marguerite would matriculate at one of the schools for
the upper crust of black society, for even then the black state colleges had
not been brought to the level of prestige and respectability of the better
financed private ones.[7] Her parents (Fred and Marguerite Rogers) were
graduates of Shaw.[8]

Although Marguerite Howie was very interested in the uplift of the
black people, there is little evidence of her strong involvement until after
the 1960s. There was still some reservation within black society that phenotypes such as Howie were truly interested in the group by their seeking
to create a culture for themselves; however, it would be most difficult for
blacks without their phenotypes to enter. The 1960s, more than any other,
clarified for persons of mixed ancestry where they would need to cast
their loyalties and efforts. Until that time, they had resided in the "land of
ambiguity," most commonly opting out of close association with the daily
problems of black Americans, though they often worked with the poor-
est of them. And yet, even before and after the Civil Rights Movement
got underway, there was still some ambiguity as to what should be the
program of the blacks of nearly white background.[9] At one college, in the
late 1940s and early 1950s, a passable faculty member, accompanied his
auburn- haired wife, more passable than himself, to the "Deep South." He
wore a different costume, did not speak, and was therefore able to escape
notice as a black man. Such persons were not unusual on the black college
campuses; especially the closer they were to their starting dates and on up
to World War 1.

A class of yellow people literally dominated black society, a domination
that did not yield until after the mid-1950s. This color cleavage within
black society caused much trouble, for it had become difficult to evaluate
individuals without dragging in the color component. Richard Wright
utilized the problem of color in his construction of the life of Bigger
Thomas. Wright's work was biographical, to a large extent, and there is a
hint in analyses of Wright's work that Wright did not think that he should
be exposed to the same problems of black Americans, since he was not

phenotypically a dark person.[10] The reactions of persons who were not phenotypically dark, often called mulattoes, quadroons, or octoroons, against the imputed caste status of all blacks has been noted from the Plessy decision of 1896 forward. Perhaps because of the relatively smaller number of yellow persons, compared to the much larger proportion of darker ones, the position of the yellow people has been more ambivalent, at least in their minds.[11]

It must have been very hard for Marguerite Rogers to make it through college fighting the stereotype commonly faced by persons such as herself. The sociological category made well known by Everett Stonequist, called the marginal man,[12] had some currency during the years of socialization of Marguerite Rogers. It is pointed out at many places in the footnotes by Myrdal that mulattoes did not have the highest verbal standing within black society, although it was thought that they did.[13] When Marguerite was in college, the Civil Rights Movement had not yet been born and her ambiguity was severely tested. Pretty girls such as Marguerite could not easily exercise their talent for having to fight off males who were determined to wreck their futures. Mulatto, quadroon, and octoroon girls were extremely vulnerable to the advances of men of all stations and races, and they probably had the least amount of socially approved protection. Many of these girls simply gave up, chose dark-skinned partners—often those without great promise for academic, professional, or business accomplishment—began their families and clarified their status. Status clarification was as important as anything else, for it meant that the ambiguously classified person could now concentrate on other aspects while gaining a precarious niche in a recognized group.

There was literally no framework for ambiguously placed blacks, especially those of the ordinary classes, to exert their leadership in group uplift. Perhaps the most rational choice for these persons was to capitalize upon their ambiguous status by securing more schooling so that they could qualify for the better jobs that were open to black people. As a result, the higher schools, collegiate and professional, for a long time contained disproportionately larger numbers of lighter-skinned black people as they scrambled for the few jobs above common labor that were open to them. Their main competition was with other black people. Although they had to become competitive, the preparation they had generally gave them an advantage in the competition much to the chagrin of the blacks of darker skin who were emerging out of lower class families and backgrounds. Howie states: "My expression of interest in black people became more vocal when I moved from the secondary school system in Charleston to the collegiate level in 1957."[14]

3
Marguerite Howie and the Association of Social and Behavioral Scientists

For more than 30 years she was an annual attendee at the meetings of the Association of Social and Behavioral Scientists. Before that the organization was called the Association of Social Science Teachers. Robert Moran, the Association Historian, writes:

> On October 26, 1935, a group of black social science teachers was invited by Dean Theophilous McKinney, of Johnson C. Smith University, to attend a conference to deliberate and suggest plans, methods, and procedures leading towards the improvement of social science offerings in black colleges.[1]

Fifty-two delegates registered at the meeting. In attendance at that meeting were Ralph J. Bunche and Charles Wesley, of Howard University, W.E.B. Du Bois, of Atlanta University, Bertram Doyle, of Fisk University, A. Ogden Porter, Lawrence D. Reddick of Dillard University, Benjamin Quarles, of Morgan State College, and Merle Tate.[2]

History has shown that there was a core of very distinguished social scientists in attendance. Some of this group made very significant scholarly contributions over their generally long careers. The proceedings of the conference were to be published in the *Quarterly Review of Higher Education Among Negroes.*[3] It was made up mainly of black teachers at the high school and college levels who felt a need to carry on professional and social life within a society which rejected even the symbol of black intellectual achievement, that is, recognition of black scholars who were working and studying in the same fields as majority ones. Dean Theophilous McKinney called the meeting in the depth of the Great Depression and at the height of the application of the Plessy v. Ferguson philosophy, which forced black people to establish a separate society, if they intended to have any at all. The euphemistic and accepted social science concept used by the majority scholars was that of "parallel development." All understood, of course, that meant second class black development, more specifically, underdevelopment. What Walter Rodney said about how Europe under-developed Africa[4] could be said for America. A book entitled *How America Underdeveloped Black America* would not be inappropriate. Not only were the majority of black people ensconced in Southern living then, but a large proportion of them were located in sharecropper and the lowest roles in common labor. Most were not even voting in the majority of the South. No black person in the South had a public position higher than that of president of a black college. Almost none were in jobs that required that they supervise majority group members. Educational jobs were among the best that could be held from the state level down to the lowest local levels. At the top of the state jobs were the presidents of the state colleges. Then came the State Supervisor of Negro Education. He worked through the local principals of black schools. These principals were perhaps the leading members of local black society. They literally controlled who was employed on a year to year basis in the black schools. They did not have absolute control for city or county superintendents of education could either recommend teachers or counter the recommendations of teachers put forward by the principals. Since the education of black youth was not a great concern of typical Southern majority educators, the recommendations of the black principals meant practically automatic employment by the candidates, if the money were available.

The Smith-Hughes, or practical skills teachers, representing essentially agricultural and home economics fields, were paid partly through funds from the federal government and so these teachers were not completely subservient to the demands and control of the principal. Principals laid off these persons whose salaries were very close to, and sometimes exceeded those of the principals.

In larger cities there were physicians, dentists, preachers, and businessmen who vied for status within black society. Although their status was often high, it seldom exceeded that of the educators, taken as a group. Their struggle for status was so great that, in many cases, they were unable to keep up their professional knowledge and their antics and activities became the bases of widespread community gossip. It did not make much difference, however, because these persons had virtually total control over black society. Some underworld persons who made livings sublegally and illegally could not be totally excluded from black society for they had the living styles and connections to demand recognition. Oftentimes all the pretenders to high black status traveled to other towns and cities where they were not known so that they could participate in activities which they would be criticized for engaging in at home.

Young people understood the trajectories they needed to follow, the people they needed to know, and the schools they needed to attend, to make their moves toward inclusion in the black social structure of their towns and in the state at large. Schools attended, whether high school or college, were important. In large cities, where there were more than one black high school, the schools were ranked from high to low. Washington, D.C. had its Dunbar and Booker T. Washington Schools. Chicago had Washington and DuSable. Memphis, Tennessee, had Sumner and Washington Schools. Cities like Atlanta, Georgia, had high schools connected to each of the several colleges, all of which were ranked according to the quality of the alumni, the students, and endowments. If there were not several schools in a city, the schools that did exist took on rankings similar to those already in existence. The best schools in the county and state were known and students from those schools were expected to do better than those from poorer schools. Expectations were not always met, perceptions were often as important as reality. On a national scale, the important schools to attend were prestigious white schools of the North, first. A black family would be happy to send its children, if girls, to any of the Seven Sisters Colleges: Smith, Wellesley, Radcliffe, Mt. Holyoke, Swarthmore, Bryn Mawr, and Sarah Lawrence, for example, or those similar. Boys who attended any of the Ivy League schools: Brown, Harvard, Yale, Pennsylvania, Rutgers, Cornell, Columbia, etc., would be highly respected and expected to immediately move to the head of the lines in terms of any privileges and recognitions that were to be offered in black society. Below them were the most important black schools. Spelman, Fisk, Hampton, Bennett, and Talladega, were the cream of the private schools, followed by Howard, Morehouse, and Lincoln University of Pennsylvania. Prestige fell off somewhat but it was always respectable to attend a number of the better black private and state colleges to be found throughout the South and in some Border states. The social structure of black society was quite similar whether it was found in the North or the South, East or West.

Elaboration of the social structure is always in process and criteria for participation are not fixed. After the end of slavery, when black people began to have a chance to build their society, the most important factor was literacy. The former slaves who had taught themselves to read, or were taught by others to do so, were oftentimes employed as teachers. Then a school district could be established with as few as twenty property holding families contiguously located. A large proportion of the small funds they paid for property taxes were used to defray the expense of a primary grade teacher. The literally thousands of these small school districts provided employment for thousands of teachers and laid the basis for the growth of the black normal or teacher colleges.

There was always the claim that the black teachers were not properly qualified and they were required to attend all manner of short courses, summer institutes, and other training in order to stay employed. In some Southern and Border states black towns were incorporated.[5] These towns determined their own school districts and there was considerable jockeying by candidates to fill the jobs of principals and teachers. The largest landholder, businessmen, farmers, and professionals made up the school boards and often were somewhat heavy-handed in determining that their friends received the few jobs that were available.

It was only in the 1950s that the majority of Southern states required a bachelor's degree for employment as a teacher. Since the 1950s, the requirements for teachers have constantly been raised through the use of higher formal degree requirements, higher grade point averages from undergraduate school for entry into teacher training, and through the use of teacher tests before hiring. The outcome is that black teachers are being gradually erased from employment in schools in which large percentages of black students are enrolled.[6]

Schools of the South, including the colleges, vied with each other for recognition, the best of the small number of qualified staff members, and for the brightest of the students available. Academic status of students was important but there was no real emphasis given to their prior test scores. Most of the schools required only a high school certificate for entry and then the school from which they entered did not need to belong to the regional or even state rating agencies, such as the Southern Association of Secondary Schools and Colleges, or the North Central Association of Secondary Schools and Colleges. What a student accomplished in college was far more significant than what his entering test scores were.

On the campuses themselves professors were isolated from their disciplines. They taught large numbers of students in the general courses and received only a little relief when students reached the upper division courses and their numbers dropped substantially. In many courses of the natural sciences it was difficult to find enough students to carry on classes. Had there been number requirements for the opening of classes there would have been many fewer blacks in the technical fields than there are now because those classes would have been canceled. In those years, before the 1970s. or so, professors were paid largely without respect to the number of students they taught. With increasing accountability it became a requirement that a number of students be enrolled in courses of certain numbers in order that those courses be continued. At black colleges such a requirement would have devastated science departments which had to deal with students who had inadequate backgrounds from high school. The few students who persisted in the scientific fields might get what could be thought of as private tutoring from the professors, but usually they received minimal education and had to rely upon their own ingenuity and brightness in order to strengthen their backgrounds. Even when they went to graduate schools with outstanding records of achievement from black colleges, they were not seen as being exceptionally bright, for the training they received was viewed as substandard. Like their counterparts in the social sciences, the natural science trainees for advanced degrees generally had to spend several years or semesters strengthening what the majority universities perceived as inferior backgrounds. With those degrees they could secure jobs immediately. Members of the black bourgeoisie could afford to send their children to the better schools where they gained background improvement and were able to move more readily into the scientific fields which were then more lucrative in terms of pay and recognition even on black campuses than degrees in the less quantitative fields. The vast majority of black students were not willing to undergo the extra years of training in order to make up for background deficiencies and so diverted into the social sciences and education.

Trying to maintain a vehicle for professional advancement forced many of the black faculty members to band together into organizations which they perceived as meeting their professional needs. Probably the first organization to which the majority of educated blacks belonged was the state teacher association. These organizations were begun under the leadership of Booker T. Washington, who saw a need to advance and control black teachers by having them address common problems. Ostensibly, they were concerned with methods which led to better instruction of the students and the application of the latest techniques of teaching. The teaching model was that which had been used in agricultural work promoted by the land-grant college movement. Teachers were to engage in continuing education, use the methods of demonstration, and even experimentation for better results in the field of education. Some of these goals were reached but the state teacher organizations soon became more than organizations for educational betterment but moved toward vehicles for the exertion of individual leadership and recognition in the state. Nascent political agendas were formulated which were aimed at wresting some concessions from the majority educational establishments which controlled their livelihood.[7]

It was necessary that teachers with common interests join together to address common goals. McKinney thought that the social science teachers in the Southern black colleges, and the larger high schools, could pool their resources and form an association which was called the Association of Social Science Teachers. At their annual meetings they read papers, almost none of which were published in the majority journals. Carter G. Woodson had established the *Journal of Negro History* in the 1920s, which allowed some outlet for black scholars interested in historical research and writing. Howard University opened the *Journal of Negro Education* around the same time and Atlanta University, under the social science leadership of W.E.B. Du Bois, established *Phylon: The Journal of Race and Culture.* These journals were practically monopolized by the scholars at the larger and more recognized schools. Those at the hinterland schools were left out. The Social Science Teachers began to publish a fifth journal, the *Journal of Social Science Teachers*, which expanded opportunities for aspiring scholars to continue their professional growth by publishing in this journal[8] However, with small budgets and uncertain funding, these journals were unable to publish more than an average of about 20 articles per journal per year, or something fewer than 100 articles per year. With a few scholars monopolizing these journals, the rank and file of black teachers and scholars felt that it was useless to continue professional growth and sought advancement and recognition through the social avenue.

Most of these journals had adopted the styles of the majority journals and addressed essentially the same types of problems, with the provision that they pertained to Negro or black subjects. Because there was little recognition of black scholarship, publication in these organs did not have much merit. Productivity in the black schools could be threatening to the school leadership, for if a scholar were known he or she might be picked up by a better black school, or occasionally a majority school in some other part of the country. Administrators reasoned that it was best to give little attention to published scholarship at their schools and only occasionally did they even permit articles and books written by blacks, whether on their campuses or off, to be reviewed on their campuses. The perception was that they did not want to antagonize the sources of funding for their schools and so the issue of scholarship could be played down. At Tuskegee George Washington Carver had made a sterling reputation in science research from around the turn of the century. His research was considered practical and for the benefit of the entire citizenry of the South and the rest of the country. It did not suggest or call for changes in the social structure as would be done by social science research. In the majority of the black schools neither scientific nor social research gained any kind of hearing. Neither administrators nor students took the scholars seriously. The idea had been set that the best scholarship came from scholars of the majority group and that a good education meant as little black instruction as possible. The black journals were accordingly tossed aside, as were black written books. The outstanding survey research of Charles S. Johnson, the sociologist at Fisk University, the research of W.E.B. Du Bois, at Atlanta University, and that of Carter G. Woodson, Rayford Logan, and E. Franklin Frazier at Howard University, and at a few other schools, even if recognized by the majority scholars, was downplayed at the black institutions. Such research stood a chance of being misunderstood by the students and might serve to antagonize the funding sources of the schools.

There was not a critical mass of black social scientists within the schools and the few scholars there were intimidated because of job insecurity. Knowing the need for research on nearly every aspect of black community life, the Association of Social Science Teachers organized a student section, ostensibly for the purpose of mentoring the students in the methods of conducting social science research. The natural sciences had an organization called Beta Kappa Chi, which promoted a scientific attitude among students at black colleges. The general liberal arts and sciences promoted Alpha Kappa Mu, which black students thought to be the counterpart of Phi Beta Kappa. The social sciences, not willing to allow recognition to leave them, countered with Sigma Rho Sigma, sounding suspiciously like Social Research Society, sponsored essentially by the Social Science Teachers Association. The hope was that black students would learn theory and methodology which they could apply to research on the black community. It was thought that they would use this knowledge to gain greater consideration in their quests for higher degrees at majority institutions in which they would need to enroll

Because keeping up with students required a good fund of physical energy, the most youthful faculty members were first given this task. Marguerite Howie began her long tenure with the Social Science Teachers Association first by working with the students in Sigma Rho Sigma. She taught at South Carolina State College and carried students to the Association meetings where they read their papers and usually received whatever monetary or other recognition as were available as encouragement. Howie became identified with Sigma Rho Sigma, the student wing of the Social Science Teachers Association.

4
Association's History and Politics

The story of the Association of Social and Behavioral Scientists may be that of black social scientists to earn recognition in their fields and personal satisfaction through the process of academic achievement. At the same time it is the story of conflicts between black social scientists for control of the minds of the students they taught and for influence in their areas. The Association was not patronized by the most notable of the black social scientists of the time, which says something about the options that individuals had who gained notoriety in the field from majority sources. Du Bois was never president of the association and neither were Charles S. Johnson, Ira de Reid, and E. Franklin Frazier, to name just a few of the notable social scientists of the time after the Association was founded. The Association itself was begun out of the recognition of the social scientists of fundamental needs of a people who cherished academic work but who wanted to make it relevant to the improvement of the lives of a rejected people. W.E.B. Du Bois' doctoral thesis at Harvard, entitled *Suppression of the African Slave Trade* (1895), signaled the rising interest of black scholars in studying their own communities and their problems always with a view to assisting them to improve from their generally unenviable conditions. Formal social science germane to the black community had been carried out since Du Bois' work in 1899 entitled *The Philadelphia Negro*. After Du Bois black scholars began a trend of studying some feature of black society. This was not unexpected since they were shackled by regimes which forbade their recognition in the mainstream disciplines. Of the noted black scholars, E. Franklin Frazier (1895-1962) was no doubt the most active in gathering data and reporting on the black community. He began his work in the early 1920s, during the period of the Black Renaissance.[1] Ironically, Frazier's sociology sought to explain black society in terms of its pathological features, essentially the same as majority scholars were doing. He thought in terms of the destruction of African society in the diaspora and the reduction of blacks, now former slaves, to persons whose behavior was essentially a lower class version of mainstream culture.

Frazier's sociology never excited black students or teachers for it seemed to justify the lower placement of black people by noting their deviations from mainstream societal norms. It was more widely accepted by mainstream scholars and served to buttress their own opinions of black society. Although Frazier was well aware of the discrimination that blacks faced in every part of the nation, he generally was not critical of the overall society. At Atlanta University, according to G. Franklin Edwards, some of Frazier's writings were viewed as threatening by the majority establishment and Frazier had to leave town in order to avoid trouble with those who did not appreciate his reasoning. After that incident Frazier became even less critical of majority treatment of blacks. His studies became more and more mainstream and critical of black people themselves as they tried to adjust to the realities of discrimination and lost opportunity.

Frazier's hostility toward black academics is revealed in his low degree of participation in their professional organizations. The present association is merely illustrative of Frazier's attitude toward such groups. When the Association of Social Science Teachers was formed in 1935, Frazier was a young man in the prime of his observational powers. There is no evidence that he participated in the association though he was teaching in schools which would have made that possible. He had by then amassed a considerable bibliography of work on the black experience and it would have seemed that he would have been a natural participant. His name does not show up in the list of association presidents though it is known that he was by then a notable social scientist. In fact, perhaps the most notable social scientist in the list of presidents up until the death of Frazier was Charles Wesley, erstwhile historian, author, college president, A.M.E. vice-bishop, and president of Alpha Phi Alpha Fraternity. The other presidents were less well-known on a national scale, even among black scholars. Some of them wrote books and a few articles but they did not achieve the recognition that Wesley received.[2]

The type of social science which Frazier conducted was a function of the training he had received, both in theory and in orientation. His most aggressive biographer, G. Franklin Edwards, has chronicled Frazier's own answering of the questions about his theoretical orientations. William Fontaine wrote an article, "Social Determination in the Writings of Negro Scholars," in which he noted that Frazier, among other black scholars, favored environmental explanations, and not biological and hereditary ones. Frazier's response to Fontaine suggests the very point we make. Frazier states:

It is not difficult to explain the outlook of the Negro scholar and the conceptual tools which he utilizes. If . . . the Negro scholar has arrived, he has become only a competent thinker and craftsman. The techniques and conceptual tools which he uses have been acquired during the course of his education. Doubtless, he has made some worthwhile contributions in the various fields, but so far he has not broadened our own intellectual vistas or forged new conceptual tools. That the Negro psychologists and social scientists are environmentalists simply means that they have taken over the viewpoint prevailing today.[3]

That Frazier was a little contemptuous of the pretensions of some black scholars who talk or write about black problems is revealed in his statement in the above quote about those scholars who have "arrived." By this he probably meant that they must have gained some recognition within the larger discipline, which further means that they needed to be legitimated by majority scholars. With that attitude it is not unexpected that Frazier would not participate to any great extent in such organizations as the Association of Social Science Teachers for when the group was founded Frazier was moving toward the pinnacle of recognition for his own studies of black life. He had already published prolifically since 1922 in such journals as the *Southern Workman*, *Opportunity*, *Social Forces* and the *Journal of Negro Education*. His articles began to appear in the major sociological journals in the early 1930s. His the *Negro Family in Chicago* (1932) established him as a major observer of black life in which he demonstrated his obedience to the theory and procedures of the Chicago School. His *The Free Negro Family* was published the same year at Nashville, Tennessee. During the very year that the Association of Social Science Teachers was founded, Frazier was showing considerable activism in scholarship about black people. He did not seem inclined to bring his talent and enthusiasm to the Association.[4]

Perhaps Frazier did not need the Association for he was gaining some recognition in the majority associations, having served as President of the Eastern Sociological Society and having published books and in the prestigious journal of the discipline.

Another notable sociologist of the early association years was Charles S. Johnson. We have already pointed out that Johnson, also one of the predominant black social scientists of the early years, was not active in the Association of Social Science Teachers after its founding in 1935. Richard Robbins, a biographer of Johnson, notes, quoting from St. Clair Drake, that Johnson worked with white social scientists in the South who were men of reasonable good will but who were extraordinarily obtuse, who did careful research but never questioned the ideology of racial segregation, or if they questioned it maintained silence above its devastating consequences.[5]

From the 1920s Johnson had been gathering data on blacks on the farms as sharecroppers. Johnson's work at Fisk University established him as a leading black sociologist and attracted the attention of some of the most notable sociologists of the majority mainstream. Robert E. Park, later chairman of the Department of Sociology at the University of Chicago, was a strong supporter of the sociology of Charles S. Johnson. The theory advocated by Johnson was that of a black caste which he had learned at the University of Chicago, that being the prevailing theoretical orientation of the time. Johnson did not need the Association in the way that prominent scholars of today do not need black associations. They gain their recognition from the mainstream and doing so may be extremely critical of the work that less notable black scholars are doing.

Charles G. Gomillion, of Tuskegee Institute (later Tuskegee University), is noted for his activism which led to the U.S. Supreme Court decision Gomillion v. Lightfoot, 1960, in which gerrymandering for the purpose of the exclusion of groups from participating in the political processes was outlawed.[6] Gomillion was once active in the Association of Social Science Teachers but his participation dropped off such that after the success of Gomillion v. Lightfoot, he did not return to the Association.

Again, the pattern is clear. Prominent black social scientists preferred not to be associated too closely with black organizations and especially with those which were attempting to promote social science understanding of the black community.

Ralph Hines has brilliantly described the problems and orientations of black social scientists. Echoing the Chicago School teaching of Robert E. Park, he thinks they have been cast into positions of marginality in that they not only gather data beneficial to the erection of theoretical frameworks, but they must do so as members of a rejected and stigmatized group, even within the professions they practice.[7]

Of the early cohort of black sociologists and social scientists who did not participate in the Association, O.C. Cox is conspicuous. Cox was handicapped by polio in both legs and had trouble moving around. Without physical mobility he was limited in the extent to which he could be involved. But Cox was not critical of black society in the way that some of the first generation members were. His aloofness from it was a function of his state of health. His work was not the kind which gained him status and recognition within the mainstream groups. He remained critical of capitalism and its inclination to take advantage of the down position of black people.

It is not only that the early participants in the Association were marginal to the mainstream disciplines. The fact is that they were not taken seriously. A few persistent writers such as E. Franklin Frazier and Charles

S. Johnson were recognized by some of the social scientists of the main-stream. But there was not enough recognition to go around and other options had to be found.

The Association of Social Science Teachers therefore became an organization of people who were not very well-known in the field but who were fairly well-known within the black social science orbit. The more notable people such as Du Bois, Frazier, and Johnson had outlets for their work while the strictures of segregation severely limited the performance and achievements of the majority of black scholars wherever they were located.

The schools at which the notable early scholars worked were among the most prestigious in the country at the time. Du Bois was favorably placed at Fisk and Atlanta Universities. Frazier, for a time was at Atlanta University and for long years at Howard University.[8] Johnson was at Fisk. Additionally, Du Bois and Johnson had gained notoriety for their work in other than purely academic contexts. As the editor of the *Crisis* and Executive Secretary of the NAACP, Du Bois was in an enviable position to become noted for his observations and insights. Almost automatic recognition came to Frazier by virtue of his association with Howard University, undoubtedly the most comprehensive of the black institutions of higher learning. Location as a professor there placed almost any individual in a good position to become noted, not only in a field, but to members of the national government as well. Opportunities came to Howard faculty members where those in the hinterlands were absolutely excluded.

Nashville, Tennessee was a good place to work and from which to gain recognition. The presence of Fisk University and Meharry Medical School and, to a smaller extent, Tennessee State University, provided opportunities for black scholars to come to the attention of wider audiences. It was probably Meharry Medical School (hereafter Meharry Medical College) that made Fisk University most recognized. That school, just across the street from Meharry, could piggy-back upon the status that was being accorded to Meharry. Medicine was the most prestigious of professions in black society, as well as within the mainstream, and Meharry was producing a large proportion of doctors for placement in black and Third World societies. Parents sent their children to Nashville so that they would enhance their possibilities for association with the most prestigious members of black society of the future.

The Association of Social Science Teachers was open to scholars across the social sciences, but those who were amassing reputations through their writings, and coming to recognition within majority scholastic circles, did not feel compelled to associate with black scholars of lesser recognition who participated in the Association. John Hope Franklin, the noted historian, was not a big participant and neither was Benjamin Brawley, the historian of Morgan State. There was perhaps a lower degree of participation of scholars from the most notable schools than from those least notable. Howard University had probably the lowest participation of all the schools even though it had the most facilities and the largest and perhaps best trained social science staff.

The Association of Social Science Teachers was begun at a time when sociology itself was in considerable turmoil. The University of Chicago dominated sociological study through the first third of the 20th century. The *American Journal of Sociology* was the official organ of the association and was published at the University of Chicago. The domination of the department at Chicago was summarized and generally known as the "Chicago School." In the 1930s, the discipline began to expand, embracing numerous scholars with special interests. Subfields were developed at a great rate. Intra-field squabbling occurred and the discipline became factionalized. In 1936, there was such hostility in the field that the American Sociological Association decided to publish an independent journal, the *American Sociological Review*[9] The internecine fighting in the discipline carried over to the black sociologists as well, for there were arguments over theory and methodology being debated within the mainstream. Black scholars were not united on what they should teach their students, especially about issues of race relations. They could not settle for the accommodationism of Booker T. Washington or the radicalism of W.E.B. Du Bois, which some considered too dangerous. Caste theory advocated by the Chicago School seemed based on the biologism and Darwinism that had been promoted by many of the scholars of the mainstream.[10] It was not acceptable, but there was no forum for objection to these teachings. The American Sociological Association was not receptive to the participation of black scholars during the 1930s, although a few were accepted if their thoughts and writings accorded with those of the mainstream. Allison Davis, St. Clair Drake, Horace Cayton, Charles S. Johnson, Ira de A Reid, and E. Franklin Frazier, then young men in the profession, did not strongly object to the caste hypothesis and thought black people would make progress to the extent that they modified their behavior in the direction of the majority group.

Formation of an alternative organization called the Association of Social Science Teachers, in 1935, although not specified as such, might have had as much to do with escaping the teachings of those black sociologists who purveyed mainstream theory as finding opportunities for their professional growth. Mainstream theory solidified blacks in their low positions by pressing the value of culture, expectations, and other means that portended very slow change in the general position of black people.

Charles U. Smith

Because the early outstanding black sociologists were not openly critical of the interpretations of majority scholars, relative to the positions of
black people, their sociology was not widely endorsed on the campuses.
When the Association of Social Science Teachers was formed, the noted
black scholars generally did not offer their wholehearted endorsement of
it. The new scholars who would develop within the Association would
contradict the leadership assumed by the scholars by now endorsed by
mainstream sociology. This undoubtedly is one reason that the most noted
black scholars were not great participants in the work of the Association.
The Association of Social and Behavioral Scientists became more than an
academic group. Yet, it never had the fullest support of black academics, even in the black colleges. There may be important reasons for this.
These schools have always had very small budgets for travel. What travel
funds as existed usually went to the college presidents and a few departmental chairpersons. Unless a meeting were in the city where the college
was located, or very nearby, the majority of black scholars were unlikely
to attend because of cost. Additionally, there was the matter of teaching
schedules which did not entertain much flexibility. Because of the heavy
teaching schedule of fifteen hours often, with only the privileged members
teaching twelve hours or less, a faculty member was likely to teach every

day. Each day missed would mean literally dozens of students would be deprived of that subject matter. Administrators were not always encouraging of faculty members to take time off from teaching and advising and so there were very few opportunities for professional growth.

There have been many treatises on the problems and prospects of the black college. Charles U. Smith, former president of the Association, was one who criticized the writings of majority figures on black colleges. Works by such scholars as David Reisman and Christopher Jencks,[11] were extremely critical of such colleges. Smith, however, recognized the difficulties under which black scholars at these institutions worked. The physical and emotional conditions were not conducive to scholarship. Smith noted that isolation, small budgets, and paternalism, eroded the energies of the scholars there. The president was head of the college family and his wife the mother. The faculty and staff were their children who would be rewarded if "good" and penalized if "bad."[12] Usually, the college was not bureaucratic enough that trips and other activities were taken care of by that process. Instead, a faculty member might be compelled to plead his or her case before a department chairperson who, in turn, would approach the president or his representative with a request that a faculty member travels. Occasionally, if the faculty member were in good standing with the president, he or she could approach the president directly. Since the college was generally chronically short of funds, the most general outcome was that a member could not travel, if he or she could not pay for the trip. Even if the funds could be scraped up, the matter of leaving the students for a few days had to be considered.

Moreover, since the typical black college was more a teaching institution than a research one, most faculty members were not expected to be on the front lines of knowledge production. Knowledge production was encouraged in only a few schools, and then mainly by scholars in the natural sciences. The example of George Washington Carver at Tuskegee illustrates the attitude of the administration and the majority controllers of the institution toward research by black scholars. The idea-changing scholarship of black social scientists would be challenged by administrators fearful of the impact of social science scholarship upon the economic controllers of the institution. It was considered wisest by administrators not to recognize social science scholarship and to assure that social science scholars did not put radical thoughts into the heads of the students. As has been noted by several writers, scholarship which was not supportive of the status quo could be severely punished by administrators, at least according to perception. The fact is that there were very few black scholars dismissed from their institutions for what they said or wrote. Part of the reason for their being ignored was that the institutions themselves were isolated and few paid attention to what was being said by the scholars there so long as no issues were made of their statements or writings. At one predominantly black college, one of the most controversial and scholarly of the social scientists was never invited to give a public lecture on his works, nor were these classic works ever reviewed in the campus or town newspapers. Perhaps since as early as the late 1940s social science knowledge had to be downgraded in all the schools, including majority ones, if that knowledge did not fit into the prevailing paradigms endorsing separation and inequality of black Americans. This is why such scholars as Daniel Patrick Moynihan,[13] Andrew Greeley,[14] Gunnar Myrdal,[15] Murray and Herrenstein,[16] William Shockley,[17] and Arthur Jensen[18] were so bitterly criticized by black scholars. Their work tended to degrade black people thereby becoming tools of those who would continue to oppress them.

The few journals that existed were more likely to be monopolized by the persons who had more notoriety or standing in the field. Thus, even with the founding of the Association of Social Science Teachers, there was no quantum jump in the rate of participation of social science scholars in the black colleges. Robert Moran notes that the Association of Social Science Teachers was open to all social science teachers whose institutions paid a $5.00 annual fee.[19]

The Focus of the Association

Several reasons might be advanced for the existence of the Association of Social Science Teachers. We have already noted that a major purpose was to break the isolation of the teachers of social sciences at the black schools. It was one way of promoting professional status within a very restricted context. Another purpose was to promote association and interaction among the members. Very strong friendships developed among the membership even as it changed over the years. Marguerite Howie is only one of the members who were almost religious about attending the Association meetings. She probably had not missed a meeting in more than 30 years. And at the meetings were some of the most vociferous and stimulating disputations of faculty members. Some of these discussions went on after the day's meetings and on into the night in hotel rooms and in hospitality suites. Generally, after the disputes over theory, methodology, the black problem in its myriad features, the members could relax, unwind, and still be friends. Thus, the Association was more than an academic organization with a set of goals to be accomplished during the several days of formal meetings annually. People seemed to matter in the Association and were valuable to it. When members missed meetings there was considerable concern for why they did so.

Cliques did develop in the Association and some of these promoted political agendas relative to the Association members. Two important rewards could be gained from the Association. The first of these was publication in the *Journal*, although it was refereed organ. For some years decisions were made by the editor as to what articles would be published in the *Journal*. There were severe limitations on the amount of funds available for journal publication. Ordinarily a school at which the editor resided subsidized the journal by making available secretarial and editorial help. This allowed a certain degree of arbitrariness on the part of the editor who could reward those persons of his choice by publishing that person's articles. The number of articles being submitted from the members of the Association was not all that great and sometimes an editor had to go to extraordinary lengths to see that enough material was available to constitute an issue. Since there were not too many advantages accruing to members at black schools from research and publication in the journal, most members did not compete.

The second reward was receipt of the W.E.B. Du Bois Award. This award was suggested by James Conyers in 1969 and was to honor some well-known black social scientist for exemplary work in the field. A luncheon on Friday of the meeting week was set aside as the Du Bois Award Luncheon. The awardee was to speak at the luncheon and receive the award which was a plaque. Among the other criteria for receipt of the award, was membership in the Association. Since the membership fee was minimal, individuals who did not ordinarily attend the annual meetings were eligible to receive the award. The first recipient of the Du Bois Award was Oliver Cromwell Cox, in 1970. After Cox a list of distinguished individuals received the award. They, including Cox, are as follows:

1970	Oliver C. Cox
1971	Lewis Wade Jones
1972	Horace Mann Bond
1973	Charles U. Smith
1974	Vivian Henderson
1975	Elizabeth Duncan Koontz
1976	John Griffin
1977	Vincent Harding
1978	Clarence Bacote
1979	Parren Mitchel
1980	Jacquelyne Johnson Jackson
1981	James E. Conyers

1982	Margaret Walker Alexander
1983	Robert Gill
1984	Marguerite R. Howie
1985	George Breathett
1986	Delores P. Aldridge
1987	Michael Espy
1988	Joseph B. Johnson
1989	Alton Hornsby, Jr.
1990	John Moland, Jr.
1991	Lena Wright Myers
1992	Eldridge W. McMillan
1993	Butler A. Jones
1994	Gordon Daniel Morgan
1995	Frederick S. Humphries
1996	Dorothy Cowser Yancy
1997	James A. Hefner
1998	John Lewis
1999	Samuel Du Bois Cook

Over time the awardees began to come from ranks outside the social sciences. Prominence in black life came to be recognized as an acceptable criterion. The award became politicized and individuals within the Association began to vie for it by having their friends vote for them or for individuals of their choice. Occasionally, individuals whose contributions to black life lay wholly in the political realm were rewarded, usually at the insistence of some individual or small group dedicated to seeing such a person rewarded. Sometimes it was thought expedient to give the award to an individual in a city where the Association was meeting in order to enhance attendance at the luncheon and to encourage membership in the Association. When the meetings were held in a particular city, participation in the Association was higher than when it was in other cities, obviously for the reason that local members would be spared the expense of out of town travel while claiming professional development through paper and panel presentations in the Association. The executive committee was scheduled to oversee the process by which the award was made. The usual procedure was to send out ballots to the membership sometimes in November of the year before the Spring meetings for nominations for the award. Since many new members either did not know the process or perhaps felt that awardees were already pre-selected, not all that many made suggestions. This left the members of the executive committee to wrangle among themselves for who would receive the award. A small group of committee members could literally decide who would receive the award.

There is some evidence of the circulation of the award among members of the committee. Sometimes a small group of members representing one or other of the sororities promoted their own sorors or perhaps withheld the award from persons whom they did not consider theoretically or politically correct. Hard feelings were caused within the Association and some members who were denied the award who thought their work was exemplary quit the Association.

The Association and Ambivalence

After the death of Martin Luther King, Jr., the number of black faculty members on majority campuses began to grow. By the mid-1970s these members had infiltrated the other associations—state, regional, and national. Some, by the late 1970s or early 1980s, had become officers in these associations. The problem which had faced black schools following integration now faced the black scholars. Would they continue to participate in their own separate associations or would they become fully integrated into the majority associations? As the numbers of blacks in the majority associations rose, they began to recognize that they were not being taken seriously, that their research was not getting published with any degree of frequency within the major journals, and that the majority associations were not speaking to the needs of black people yet trapped in the ghettos without possibilities. In the late 1970s black scholars formed a caucus within the American Sociological Association for the purpose of prompting the American Sociological Association to address the concerns of black people who were studied frequently in articles, books, theses and dissertations. That caucus become known as the Association of Black Sociologists. Similar caucuses were established among blacks in other disciplines as well. The caucus forced the American Sociological Association to consider black scholars more generally. By the late 1980s, William Julius Wilson was elected the second black president of the American Sociological Association.

While the caucuses became installed within the majority associations of social scientists, they created competition with the older predominantly black Association of Social Science Teachers. Faculty members who would have been members of that association during the darker days of segregation found outlets in the majority associations arguing that they could receive little, or in fact might be damaged by participation in the Association. Others claimed that they did not have time to participate for the meetings of that association conflicted with the mainstream association meetings or other duties they had which awarded them status and recognition. It was held by some black members that they could not spend the time traveling to black meetings which did not meet in hub cities where air transport would not be a problem. They did not like to change to commuter planes which serviced the smaller cities without hubs. Some members refused to participate at any level in the black based associations holding that they promoted segregation, the very thing they were trying to oppose. Very prominent black social scientists boycotted the meetings and incurred the wrath of those who did attend and participate. The issue here, of course, was to whom did the black social scientists owe allegiance? Could they work in behalf of the group in this way or would their efforts be more fruitful through greater involvement in the mainstream societies? Some held that blacks in the mainstream societies were really tokens and that there was no fundamental appreciation of their work within those societies, even when they were elected as presidents or to other important and symbolic positions in those societies. They were said to be toys, to be taken on over in those societies by adoring majority members who were thrilled to be in the presence of or to be able to say that they were personal friends or acquaintances of this or that black academic star. In the black societies these persons lost their star status and could be debated head-to-head for they were not as intimidating to black social scientists as they would be in the majority societies. Partly because of the perception that blacks would be hostile toward them, blacks who had received their prominence through majority recognition further decreased their participation in activities which were largely black-based.

Although the numbers of black social scientists were higher than ever before, they were still small when their disciplines were taken as a whole. Out of some ten thousand sociologists, perhaps 1% or less were black. It was the same pattern in other disciplines for the number of blacks receiving doctoral or other advanced degrees, the basic requirement for moving into college and university teaching was not being widely met. As late as 1994, according to most competent studies, no more than 800 blacks received doctoral degrees in all fields. Those numbers had been fairly constant for ten or fifteen years. The degree holders were to be distributed over more than 3000 institutions in which such degrees were required. Many of the persons receiving degrees have been in-service and did not add "new blood" to their fields. In all the fields they were in jeopardy of being tokenized, that is, treated as employees whose status depended upon Affirmative Action instead upon the knowledge and skills they brought.

The problem, of course, was to what extent could black associations help members who were working in more mainstream institutions? This was the dilemma which faced members of the earlier group of social scientists when the Association of Social Science Teachers was formed.

No answer has yet been posed for the dilemma. There are literally hundreds, perhaps as many as 5000 black social scientists nationwide. We have no official figures, but if common observation is a guide, if the approximately 3000 institutions of higher education in the U.S. had an average of two black social scientists, representing all departments, the number would be around that which has been proposed. Many of these faculty persons were not socialized in the settings of the black schools. They were found in small numbers in the schools they attended, generally from elementary school on. Practically their entire professional exposure has been outside the traditional black experience. It is possible that they have no loyalty to, or great interest in, the realities of the black experience outside the safe confines of academia. Unless there were members on their faculties that appreciated the problems of minority faculty, these younger faculty members' interest in the problems of the education of minority youth would not expand.

Socialization and resocialization of the more youthful faculty was indeed a part of the assumed role of seasoned professors like Marguerite Howe. Yet there were limited ways by which all those who could profited from the type of socialization she offered. Even on the black campus gaps between faculty and staff members developed. One of the more serious ones was that between the senior and junior faculty members. The older faculty members, and administrators, socialized during the period of rank segregation, have held on to different agendas for approaching the majority society. They had their ways of surviving and advancing, which did not always appeal to the more youthful faculty, many of whom were socialized into the merits of direct confrontation. Since these senior persons have usually advanced into the higher positions on campus, they prove to be more difficult to remove than those younger persons located in the middle portions of teaching and administration. Unless the senior members are deeply involved in the academic work of teaching, research, writing, and other service, they may be tolerated but not highly respected by their colleagues.

The options open to the black college administrator to deal with unproductive senior faculty are not the same as are available to the majority administrator. In state institutions, funds are not as highly restricted as they are in the less affluent private schools. In the latter, persons may be removed with fewer repercussions than in the former. In majority state institutions, used-up administrators and unproductive faculty may be shunted to other duties that remove them from the direct management of students and programs of the school. Some of these persons may even be given high-sounding titles and better offices. The reality is that they have reached the level of titular performance and have essentially been removed from the daily process of teaching and research. A few black faculty members, in majority schools, and in state and private institutions, may gain some of these emoluments. Usually, the black administrator is faced with the retention of faculty members and administrators who have not been productive and who do not qualify for advancement into the distinguished professorships and chairs. If they decide to stay on until well beyond the usual dates of retirement, there is not much the black administrator can do.

5
Transcending Academics

A review of the literature on the outstanding black social scientists in black colleges tended to focus on men; yet, women were highly represented in the departments. In departments which had more than four members, half or more were usually women. When numbers reached five or more the tendency was toward a smaller proportion of women. This is the reason that the larger schools such as Howard and Morgan State, with larger social science departments, had smaller proportions of women teachers than men. More often than not, men tended to serve as departmental chairs.

Several factors need to be considered in regard to the discrepancies between the proportions of men and women in social science departments. One factor was the salary structure. There was no salary scale in the schools; vast gaps existed among and between faculty members. Pay choices were largely left to the college president who was constrained only by the total budget available. Persons with doctoral degrees were in much better negotiating positions than those without, for there was a serious shortage of those degrees among blacks generally. The pressure on the schools to achieve or maintain accreditation so that their graduates would not be penalized when they sought further study compelled presidents to be more lenient to holders of the doctoral degree. These serious salary gaps continued to exist when the data were divided by gender and, as a result, hard feelings were inevitable.

Overall, women were paid less than men even when educational levels were controlled. The women were more willing to work for lower salaries in the colleges, for there were other compensations. Black colleges were still the center of black social life, for the cities in which they were located and, often, in the region and the state. Women working in these cities had greater possibilities of coming into contact with a significant number of highly mobile black males, thus enhancing their possibilities for finding, individually, very favorable and middle class partners.

Thus, there was a greater willingness of black single women to function in the colleges as compared to men. Younger black men who remained single were often characterized negatively, by the terminology of the time; they would be considered as gays today, although that may not have been the title assigned then. Likewise, young single women, in certain fields, ran the risk of acquiring that moniker. Their singleness could best be understood as a function of their willingness to render service in the uplift of black people. Many notable black women of the earlier times did not have husbands or they did not have long and permanent marriages. They were married to their work.

Often, where there was a greater likelihood of black presidents and chairpersons to hire persons who promoted the leaders and enhanced their images, women were perhaps a greater part of the departments. The records of graduate schools show that black women were actually larger proportions of the total number of blacks receiving degrees than majority women were of their ethnicity. Black families have long offered educational preference for their female children as a buttress against the hardships they were almost sure to face in the outside world. So, as the number of black males eligible for marriage was always restricted, females ran an even higher risk of living lives of singlehood if they were highly educated, or if they required higher education of their potential marriage partners.

When women did work in academic departments, they were often overshadowed by males, even when they had equivalent credentials. One such example was Caroline Bond Stewart Day, born in 1889, in Montgomery, Alabama, who studied at Tuskegee Institute from 1901 to 1905. She attended Atlanta University from 1905-1912. Day received A.B. and A.M. degrees from Radcliffe by 1919. Working with E.A. Hooton at Harvard and, finally, through the Bureau of International Research of Harvard/Radcliffe, she completed a study of 2,537 adults from 346 families. That study was published in 1932 as *A Study of Some Negro-White Families in the United States*. After that study Caroline Bond Stewart Day taught at Howard University and was overshadowed by E. Franklin Frazier.[1] At Morgan State College is another example; Irene Diggs taught social sciences and foreign languages for years, amassing an impressive vita sheet with many international entries.[2] She was practically overshadowed by Benjamin Brawley, there as well as Frazier at nearby competitor school Howard. At Arkansas AM&N College, Ida Rowland Bellegarde, Ph.D. in social sciences from Laval University, Quebec, was so overshadowed by men, notably by Tilman C. Cothran, and other males, that she did not become a "productive scholar" until she retired in the mid-1970s. Bellegarde began her work as a creative scholar when she was a small girl, publishing poems in organs for which she received pay. Her first book of

Jackie Jackson

poems came out in 1939, making her a member of the Harlem Renaissance, notoriety for which she was never rewarded.[3] Even at the very time that the most notable black male social scientists were active, there were women in their departments or areas who were almost completely overshadowed.

When women did work in the social science departments, they were seldom expected to conduct work as scholars. Jewell Prestage obtained her Ph.D. by age 22 at Iowa State University, becoming the first black woman to earn that degree in political science in the United States. She did so in 1954. She taught for a few years at Prairie View University in Texas and moved to Southern University in Baton Rouge, Louisiana. There, her status was so low that she had to share an office with a man with much less ability and promise than herself. It is thought that she was being punished and downgraded because other women and men were envious of her achievements. A similar fate befell Jacquelyne Jackson, a later prominent scholar in the field of medical sociology, especially gerontology.

Women were punished more frequently than men by being left off the summer teaching schedules, even though it was known that they needed to work as badly as the men. They were expected more to give students basic information about their disciplines, usually handling the more generic and lower division courses. Their student faculty ratios were higher, for frequently they handled the introductory courses while the men often, even now, teach theory, methodology, and statistics. Then, as now, those are considered to be the most critical courses in the production of future social science scholars and, therefore, had to be handled by the "more scholarly men." It was and is a sad state of affairs.

Although there had been some forward movement of black women in the social sciences slightly before and following the Brown decision of 1954, black women did not begin to assert themselves in the social science fields until the late 1960s, again when changes were forced by the life and death of Martin Luther King, Jr. Soon thereafter, black women scholars began to be more noticed for work outside the fields of poetry, literature, and drama. Scholars such as Adelaide Hill Cromwell, who had been conducting research for years, began to be noticed. Of the then younger scholars, it was probably Jacquelyne Jackson, Ph.D. from The Ohio State University, 1960, who began to make a statement that women scholars had arrived. Jackson was active in the Association of Social Science Teachers and added verve and analytical acumen to the meetings. She worked at Tennessee State University and Howard, where she sharply competed for recognition with the established male hierarchy. Jackson's promise and research in the field of gerontology, along with her activism and litigiousness at Howard, made her a promising candidate for placement as a sociologist in the Medical School of Duke University.

Jacquelyne Johnson Jackson is the first prominent black woman sociologist. While a few others had received doctoral degrees before the 1920s, most were so unusual, by attainment of their advanced degrees, that they were more like celebrities than touched with the scholarly mission. Unlike other educated black women, Jackson felt that her task was that of the liberation of her people through the providing of carefully collected data that would cause blacks and others to better understand their position.

Jackson gained her underschooling at Palmer Memorial Institute, Sedalia, North Carolina, under the tutelage of Dr. Charlotte Hawkins Brown. There she was not completely in tune with the ideas that were then purveyed by leaders, such as Dr. Brown, of properly educated black people. Dr. Brown admonished her students to excel in education and manners and to "be somebody." Without saying it, Jackson suspected that Dr. Brown used the puritanical standards of New England education to inform her work with the black youth sent to her.[4]

Throughout her career, Jacquelyne Jackson distinguished herself as a serious gatherer of facts about black life, with especial emphasis on women and the aging. Her contributions to the scholarly literature through her articles, books, and commentary are notable.

Another very bright light in the field of sociology was Joyce A. Ladner, who received the Ph.D. from Washington University, St. Louis, Missouri, in 1968. Ladner's youth, independence of thought, and willingness to combine academics and activism, qualified her to teach at Brooklyn College, where she remained for some years. Later, she moved to Howard University, where she worked in sociology and administration. Ladner was never very much involved in Association work.

Lena Wright Myers, at Jackson State University, Ph.D. from Michigan State University, 1975, conducted very recognized research, most notably on the coping skills of black women. Myers has been very active in the Association, becoming its president and later recipient of the coveted Du Bois Award. Myers subsequently moved to Ohio University; she remains a strong presence in Association affairs.

Other Association women include such notables who could be cited for their work, as Delores Aldridge, at Emory University, Dorothy Cowser Yancy, Georgia Institute of Technology and, later, president of Johnson C. Smith University and LaFrances Rodgers-Rose of the University System of New Jersey. Ruth Dennis, of Meharry Medical College, Nashville, Tennessee, and Austin Peay State University, Clarksville, Tennessee, showed herself to be an able scholar utilizing the quantitative methodologies in her studies of deviance, suicidology, and prison behavior. Beverly H. Wright, now of Tulane University, Stella Hargett of Morgan State University, and Patricia McGill, of Jackson State University, Jackson, Mississippi, have shown every indication of being scholars of whom much will be heard in the near future. The Cleveland State University women, represented by such very promising scholars as Sanza Clark, Delores Lariet, Willa Hemmons, and Maggie Jackson, have made their impressions felt in the Association and on their own campus. All these women, and numerous others from other institutions, have continued to produce provocative papers and have energized the Association meetings through interpersonal relations.

Delores P. Aldridge was a president and a Du Bois awardee of the Association of Social and Behavioral Scientists. She is the first black woman ever employed at Emory University, Atlanta, Georgia, and became the first woman to ever hold an endowed chair named for a living African-American woman. She was, for a long time, the only black woman in sociology to hold an endowed chair at a major university—The Grace Townes Holmes Chair at Emory University. Her work is far-ranging, but she is a pioneer in the modern Black Studies Movement with theoretical work conceptualizing African-American Studies as an intellectual social movement.

LaFrancis Rodgers-Rose is the president and founder of the International Black Women's Congress. Among her many printed works is her edited book, *Violence Against Black Women* (1996). A provocative lecturer, Dr. Rodgers-Rose has spoken to many audiences and conferences at a variety of institutions. Her Ph.D. degree is from The Ohio State University, 1963. She has been involved in the Association for many years, and is distinguished among the past presidents.

There were other women in the Association whose contributions are notable. We are impressed with the diligence of Cynthia Hudley, of University of California, Santa Barbara, and Josephine Bradley, of Clark Atlanta University. Time dims our memories and causes us to lose our notes. There is no intention of overlooking any of the women, or men, who worked diligently to make the Association more than a yearly gathering of scholars intent on presenting their research and reading papers.

While the Association serves as a vehicle for the encouragement of scholarship among all those who wish to participate, it is especially helpful for those scholars who, because of the theses they maintain, because of their failure to endorse and promote mainstream theoretical values, usually to the detriment of the black community, remain outside of, or marginal to, mainstream attention.

Our hypothesis remains that the opening of the social science structure to general black participation means a diminution of participation of the most notable persons in black associations. In academics, this is most noticeable in the failure of black departmental chairs, deans, chancellors, presidents, and other well-known black personages and scholars, to participate in such work. Yet, as the example of Marguerite Howie illustrates, such work began, at first, as a way of becoming involved on the campuses with younger students and grew in personal importance to the individuals over the years, even when there were minimal gains to be garnered from participation. Had there not been a major change in the attitude of the country toward their greater inclusion, black women scholars would, no doubt, have continued to be overshadowed by the males determined to make their impressions on the scholastic world. Howie represented a generation when women were actually secondary to the men. When the weight of the college presidents was added to the eminence of noted males gaining recognition as scholars, it was extremely difficult for women to rise in scholastic recognition. At Fisk, no woman rose to recognition during the time of Charles S. Johnson, the eminent sociologist. No woman scholar, either in the social or natural sciences became noted while Mordecai Johnson, the president, or E. F. Frazier and John Hope Franklin, both eminent social scientists, were at Howard.

When black women began to have important roles in the social sciences, largely in their own associations or institutions, they were very group-oriented, intending that their research have some relevance to the improvement of the black condition. They followed the tradition set by the earlier generation of involved black women who were largely club and community directed. The work of Jacquelyne Rouse, *Lugenia Burns Hope*, contains much of the information on the activities of the early club women, such as Mary McCleod Bethune, Mrs. Booker T. Washington, Mary Church Terrell, and others, and illustrates the attitudes of black women toward the problem of group uplift.[5] They were rejected for a time by the traditional male establishment but, eventually, could work with males in the accomplishment of group goals. Although a young woman at the time of the notoriety of these women, Marguerite Howie became a part of that tradition. Her work was wholly compatible with that of the males with whom she was associated. For most of her professional career Howie, like most other women of her time, worked in the shadows cast by males. There was no concept of male domination as a political issue, for women were fully integrated into the arrangements and had specific and important roles to play. There was a rather clear division of labor which did not pit males and females as antagonists. Part of the division of labor provided for female protection, because some activities which were required, even of social scientists, were hazardous to females, especially in the segregated structure of the South. The campus and the local community were their domain. On campus they could work with the various clubs which chose them, or which they chose for sponsorship supplemental to their generally full teaching loads of often 15 hours of classes filled with students. They could be active in church work, if such churches were nearby or if they had transportation to reach them. If women put too much effort into church or community service, however, they could be accused of neglecting their teaching and could come under scrutiny by their chairpersons or supervisors.

Women were not expected to go unprotected into hostile areas of the South, or even in their own cities, for the purpose of gathering data. Every city in which a black college was located had areas which were off limits to young teachers, especially to female teachers and students. Quite often these areas were within the black community. Drinking places, pool halls, hangouts of persons of ill-repute, and places which served as defining lines between rough-cut farm people and the more sophisticated city people were among those off limits to educated black women. In one school the dean of women sought to protect the girls by mapping out a route for them to go to town. They were to return by the same route. Nor were they to accept rides from any males unless they were bonafide members of the faculty. These same rules applied largely to the younger female faculty members, especially if they were unmarried. Their roles may instead, center on the analysis of data which had been gathered by males. If the women were not comfortable with the roles they were expected to play, they seldom objected. Howie, thus, felt close to the men with whom she worked and enjoyed their camaraderie, while maintaining her own professional integrity.

Howie completed college in 1939, long before the Civil Rights Movement moved into high gear. Black colleges had not changed greatly in the way they were organized or in their mission to the general community. They were mainly teacher training institutions, where the emphasis was upon turning out teachers who could compete for the best jobs within the limited opportunity structure. There was such a crying need for good teachers that not a lot of emphasis was placed upon their preparation for graduate studies. In 1939, most Southern schools did not meet state and regional accreditation requirements. These same states, in general, did not require that teachers have bachelor degrees, nor was there much attention given to fields in which persons taught. Many were teaching out of their fields, not only in the lower schools, but at the collegiate level as well. There was no serious thought given at the highest levels to the quality of education which black students were to receive.

Unlike some younger women later associated with the broad movement called "Women's' Liberation," Howie never saw herself as oppressed by the males with whom she worked and, consequently, never became alienated from them. She attempted to transmit this tradition to younger students whom she was charged to instruct.

The relationship between women on the black campuses was probably no stronger than that which later existed between women and men on majority campuses in the wake of the Women's Liberation Movement. There were few women in any discipline on the campuses, a fact which militated against the growth of strong academic bonds between women. Developing strong ties across disciplines was about as hard on the black campuses as on the majority ones. There was some opportunity to mitigate these problems by work in community clubs, church work, and in the sororities, which cut across campuses and discipline lines. Similar opportunities were open to males which encouraged their involvement across discipline lines. The tendency of the presidents to forge unity within the campus by constantly referring to the institution as a family in which all had important roles to play encouraged interaction across the usual lines of division on a campus. The isolation of the black college meant that there had to be some harmony on the campuses, even though there were possibilities for great cleavages within the faculty and student bodies.

Yet, as divided as the campuses were, with foci on such factors as partying, good-timing, styling, and the continual antagonism of Greek letter societies, which carried over to an important extent to the adult college and local community, black women and black men never became antagonists. On the black campuses, it appeared counterproductive for women and men to conflict when their overall goal was the education of youth for the task of contribution to the liberation of black people.

While teaching, Howie felt a keen need to prepare students for the work they would continue when they gained responsibility. She felt that a knowledge of the history of the group was extremely important, not just knowledge of the giants of black life. Booker T. Washington, Du Bois, Wheatley, the members of the Harlem Renaissance, Martin Luther King, Jr., and others who have become a part of the black cultural pantheon, she felt, would continue to be recognized and their stature would grow. Alternatively, she felt that other persons who had not achieved the recognition of these persons had also labored long and hard in the vineyard. Howie tried to have students research within the disciplines in which they were preparing—to locate black people who had made notable contributions in those disciplines. In sociology, she asked students to search out and write papers on the work of contemporary black scholars. They were surprised to find that quite a few of them were busy studying and reporting on various phases of black and the more general society.

Marguerite Howie always had a love for learning and the expansion of the mind. She was quite research-oriented, at a time when that was not the prevailing expectation of women in the schools in which she worked. There were not all that many incentives for conducting research, nor was it widely recognized on campus. Howie understood that her choice was to fit into the woodwork as a typical teacher competing for the limited recognition available which came from the president or his representatives, or to seek to create a niche for herself based upon her understanding of and her willingness to write about the social system. Total attention could not comfortably be given to both of these tasks, so her efforts had to be divided between the two options. She understood the influence of the presidents and their representatives and she realized that there were goals that transcended the campus. She knew that if reputations were to be made, they would be made in arenas outside the campus, in professional organizations, where one's name became associated with wider accomplishments. Yet, the roles of a female and scholar provided their own boundaries for much of the life of Marguerite Howie.

Although Marguerite Howie was very active in academic and in Association work, she felt that the way to effect change was to become active at the more local level. She had been extremely sensitive to the inequalities which existed between black and mainstream Americans, while seeking their redress. She had worked avidly through the local and state branches of the NAACP. In 1991, she was a party to a suit filed against the Rowan-Salisbury Board of Education. The suit was filed in the United States District Court in Greensboro, seeking to change the residency district, numbered seat, staggered term and at-large method of election to a district system where residents of the district vote for the candidate from that district. Five members were elected from residency districts, and voted on by all county voters and two elected at-large on staggered terms. The suit charged that the procedure for electing members of the Rowan-Salisbury Board of Education had the purpose and/or effect of diluting minority voting strength. Blacks constitute approximately seventeen (17%) of the citizens of Rowan County.[6]

Blacks have had candidates for the County Board of Education, but none had been elected. Blacks served on the City Board of Education by appointment, prior to the present merged board of 1990. After merger, no blacks were elected to the present seven member board, and the present scheme impairs the ability of blacks to elect the candidate of their choice.

The dilution of black voting strength in Rowan County frustrated black voting participation.

Marguerite Howie stated:

The time is long past for deliberative bodies to affirmatively seek out and adopt voting schemes which include and not exclude. Reason, fairness and justice demand a process which allows black citizens to elect representatives of their choice.[7]

By her involvement, even in retirement, Howie showed that she yet retained a very strong social conscience.

6
Miss Howie's Challenge

When Miss Howie began her teaching career in the early 1940s the character of students had not changed appreciably for the past 50 years. Wilmoth A. Carter, et. al., write:

> Until the sixth decade of the 20th century, the traditionally Negro American college, while not devoid of student unrest, tended to have its campus dissidence directed more toward problems arising from internal management than from outside sources.[1]

The models of education were found somewhere between the accommodationism of Booker T. Washington and the ideas of W.E.B. Du Bois, which were at that time considered radical. Washington's shadow extended over practically the entire school and economic systems as then applied to black Americans. Essentially Washington had counseled that positive change would be forthcoming when black Americans decided to make indispensable contributions to the society of which they were a part. Though times were hard, they would reject welfare; they would not become discouraged; they would open businesses, accumulate property, and live conventional lifestyles. They would be models of deportment and leadership in their communities. The task of the educated black person was to lead in the development of the black community.

Du Bois and Washington were not all that far apart in terms of their hopes and dreams for the black community. In an effort to summarize the teachings of Washington and Du Bois, the tendency is to focus upon Washington's accommodationism and Du Bois' idea of the role of the "talented tenth." Du Bois and Washington were cognizant of the long tenure that blacks had in their unenviable status as slaves. The slave culture had stamped the majority of them with certain mannerisms, values, and behaviors which remained readily identifiable. Bitter controversy broke out between scholars of the African tradition school, led by Professor Melville

Herskovits, of Northwestern University, and the "obliterationist school," led by E. Franklin Frazier of Howard University.[2] Herskovits argued that Africanisms had been retained wherever there were sufficient numbers of blacks for cultural traditions to be begun or maintained. Herskovits thought that these traditions would not die even if they were suppressed for a long time. If given any opportunity parts of this culture would be resurrected and reinvented for much of the culture was invested not only with utility, but with emotion. Herskovits, therefore, became an early critic of the functionalist school which placed so much attention on culture as a rational response to societal requirements that the emotional phase of it was downgraded or practically discarded. Proof of the validity of Herskovits' thesis was found throughout the West Indies and in Southern United States where large numbers of blacks were found. It could be written many years later that the farther South one goes the closer he gets to Africa.

Frazier, schooled more in social class analysis, concluded that the behaviors of the unassimilated blacks were due to their impoverishment and placement in a lower class culture, separated from the offerings of the mainstream. Their attempts to erect institutions were thus lower class manifestations of the offering of the majority culture and had little to do with the retention of Africanisms, most of which had been obliterated during the long period of slavery. With a few exceptions these behaviors had to be practiced within a separate black society for they were not acceptable to the majority group.

The half million or so blacks who were quasi-free at the end of slavery were the ones who had better advantages to become literate, property owners, educated. They were Du Bois's "talented tenth," the group upon whose shoulders would rest the responsibility for raising the vast masses of untutored former slaves.

A resolution of the controversy between Washington and Du Bois, and continued in the Herskovits-Frazier debates had not been reached when Miss Howie began her teaching career. Because the teachings of both Washington and Du Bois laid stress upon the changes that black Americans would have to make in their own lives, of their own accord, it became clear that community development would devolve upon the people themselves. Government itself had not resolved the issue in terms of its meaning for the expanded citizenship of black people. If schooling made a difference, even within the black community, with those without it falling under the tutelage of those with it, an economic and social gap would emerge between the educated and uneducated. The educated would continue to separate from the uneducated even though these class differences would not have the consequences they had in majority society. The elaboration of conspicuous lifestyles which announced their rank within the black community became of paramount importance to the educated class. In preparing to enter that class, the concerns of the students were not so much with social change as with the achievement of individual mobility. If enough persons within any of the numerous black communities could achieve the symbols of mobility their collective achievements would enhance their opportunities for recognition by the majority community. Their status within their own community would be significantly enlarged.

Miss Howie did not enter college teaching soon after completion of her master's degree. She began teaching at South Carolina State College in 1957 at a time when the effects of the Brown decision of 1954 had not significantly affected black schools. Yet this decision, while portending the end of segregation on nearly all levels of schools, was especially threatening to black school administrators who saw that they would lose control of black students who would defect to the majority schools, secondary and collegiate. At the same time, the deficiencies of the black schools meant they could not attract ordinary white students of college age. Very serious also was the opening of teaching opportunities to blacks especially in the colleges and universities outside the South. To meet these challenges, the black colleges had to change their foci. The tendency of these schools was to try to upgrade, to offer a wider range of programs, and additional and often higher degrees. The traditional staff, schooled in the processing of students for the limited status they would hold in black society, came under attack by the students themselves. Newer, often younger faculty members and leaders were sought out who could better relate to the needs of the students. Carter et. al. write:

> . . . paternalistic Negro administrators are stifling black development by mindlessly imitating white educational methods which ignore the cultural and political needs of black people.[3]

Miss Howie's role then became one of preparing individual black students for the taking of opportunities to achieve personal mobility through the acquiring of education. At practically no level of government was there encouragement that the separate status of black Americans would be changed. Their ensconcement in their own communities would be both opportunities and limitations. On the side of opportunity there would be the reduced competition from the majority group. Black businesses could be opened in the community, property accumulated, professions promoted, along with senses of accomplishment and the development of self-esteem. Anything could be accomplished in the black community if minds, common sense, and resources from the community were devoted to the task. On the limitations side, the development of the black community only served to announce further that blacks were not recipients of full American citizenship. What they accomplished represented a diminished version of what was available within the majority community. This sense of second class citizenship would continue to gnaw at those who sharply perceived the contradictions. Yet, it was not a time to openly question the status of the group within the overall social structure. The failure to do so was not due completely to fear, reticence or intimidation. For many blacks the structure which existed made sense for those most favorably placed in black society. They would serve as models to those with aspirations to social mobility. The prevalent paradigm for blacks as well as whites was black adjustment to the status they faced with the proviso that through individual effort and initiative, and adherence to the majority norms they would be rewarded, if mainly within their own social structure.

The generation of social scientists from whom Miss Howie received her training were not radicals who counseled change, but were generally persons who had themselves accommodated to the situations they faced by avoiding confrontation with the majority society. Educated people did not go to places where they were not wanted but sought to establish alternatives of which they could be proud. This behavior could be rationalized by saying that protesting, agitating, and complaining were not signs of education. A sign of good education was to complain as little as possible about system inequalities and to work hard in the preparation of the next generation who would reap the benefits of excellent preparation. Acceptance into the majority society would be based upon the principles enunciated by Washington and the careful preparation for citizenship through exhibition of the cultural traits of the majority group, as specified by Du Bois. These were practical as well as academic or theoretical solutions to the problems faced by the group.

As the faculty members and mentors became adept at evading those conditions and circumstances which would illustrate their second class citizenship, they willy-nilly communicated this idea to their student charges. The campus became something of a cocoon—insulation from the reality faced by the black people in the work-a-day world. Practically everything that the students needed—especially those things of a social nature—was provided on the campus. The campus became an environment for the competition for status. It became the center of status striving within the black community which surrounded it. Persons who were associated with the campus became the envy of the community and sometimes hostilities broke out between campus people and non-campus persons who perceived important status gaps between the two groups.

The campus practically overshadowed the rest of the community and its institutions. Not even the major church congregations could compete with the campuses as centers of black status striving. The majority community did not know much about the daily operations of the campus. Its leaders felt comfortable with a strong president in charge, one who understood the place that blacks would hold until changes were made. The cocooning of the students encouraged their responsibility to the President and his representatives. Together they had virtually complete control over the students. They assumed responsibility for the academic, intellectual, and moral development of their students. This arrangement was generally acceptable to the students and their parents, for the concept of in loco parentis prevailed.

It is difficult to get a fix on why this situation changed. It is thought that the return to the campuses of former soldiers following World War II was instrumental in promoting the changes. It is true that the returning veterans brought with them new experiences in interpersonal relations; they were more mature, and they were practically financially independent of the colleges in a way that students had not been before. This economic independence, along with their maturity, loosened the control that the college administrators and teachers had over the students. In many schools, efforts were made to separate the veterans from the regular students by encouraging them in more mature, generally more practical curricula. This reduced their numbers in the typical liberal arts classes. In these classes, the veterans were often quieted by awarding them higher grades or excusing them from some of the work. Even so, the veterans constituted enough of a force to control some of the student leadership activities and some of the sports programs. Veterans were preferred as dating partners by many of the female students and younger female faculty members.

Overall, it probably was not the returning of the veterans which changed the character of the black college, although they no doubt contributed to that change. The very same processes which encouraged veterans to return to school encouraged the younger students to enroll. All could see that jobs were becoming more technical, more intellectual, requiring greater literacy. Agriculture was being mechanized; sharecropping was losing force as an employer of many Southern blacks. Migration to the city was in full swing and the competition for the better jobs was becoming fierce. Even if teaching remained something of a sinecure for many black college students, it was becoming clear that degrees and credentials were sure to become requirements for this level of work. Education for the black American remained the surest buttress against economic and social hardship. College enrollments were bound to grow.

With enrollment growth, which had not occurred generally since the colleges were begun, there were bound to be changes in the character of the institutions themselves. Although black parents were yet impoverished, as a category, they were more affluent than they had ever been, by the opening of the 1950s. More of them could afford to pay the way of their children to college, although the vast majority yet needed financial help. Overall, though, the students were not as strapped for cash as they were before the war and could afford to devote less attention wholly to classes and more concern to issues off the campus. Gradually there arose an understanding of the connection between social placement and the kind of schooling received. At an incipient level black students began to show some disgruntlement with the conditions their parents and communities faced, though this cannot be said for the majority of them. At a few schools where generally the more affluent black students enrolled, mainly those such as Howard, Fisk, Talladega, and perhaps Hampton, the students felt less threatened, being able to examine social issues and their consequences to a greater extent than was common in the state supported schools. Howard and Fisk were especially problematic; Howard for its standing as a federal university receiving its appropriation from the U.S. Congress and Fisk having elaborated a tradition of liberal education equal to that of some of the noted majority schools. For a long time these schools more or less set the standards for black colleges in general. The students at such schools were more difficult to manage because they were more critical. Even the teachers there encouraged their openness, to a greater extent.

We have elaborated upon the kind of social environment the black school was and some of the functions of its existence. The schools and the work of the instructors in them must be understood within the context of the times. Indeed, they were a function of those times.

In a real sense, there was no meaningful category of students called black students, or even Negro students, before the Civil Rights Movement of the 1950s. This statement seems true because there was no difference in ideology between majority students and minority ones. If anything, the minority students, and their mentors, had tried to structure the experience of their students so that they would more closely approach the norms of the majority students. Howard University, Washington, D. C., the largest, and no doubt the most influential of the black colleges, referred to itself as the "Harvard on the Potomac." Spelman College in Atlanta, Georgia, called itself "Black Radcliffe." Lincoln University, of Jefferson City, Missouri, a land-grant institution, promoted itself among its followers as the "Harvard on the Missouri." The models of these schools were Harvard or other high status institutions that gave their own an aura of distinctiveness. Within the states the schools vied for recognition. Where there were several schools, they became ranked, at least symbolically, and sometimes extreme distance developed between the schools. For instance, in Nashville, Tennessee, the gap between Fisk and Tennessee State University became so great that students from one school have been physically intimidated when they went to the other institution. For years the two schools refrained from engaging in athletic contests for fear that the respective students could not be controlled. The antagonisms between students from different institutions involved matters of class and status and there was little to meld them together with a black agenda or ideology.

The development of black students as a separate category began in the 1920s, during the period of the Harlem Renaissance. Then there was a questioning of the negativity of being black that had not been advocated under the influence of mainstream thinking. Although the model of assimilation was thought to be the operative one, reality lagged behind. An option became one of revising the attitudes then held toward themselves and the black community. There was a reaction against the stereotypes that were used to define black students and a greater appreciation of those features that gave distinctiveness to the black culture. The acquiring of the Black National Anthem, "Lift Every Voice," by James Weldon Johnson and Rosamond Johnson, began to unify black people as never before. The dialect writings of some of the more notable of the Renaissance writers, such as James Weldon Johnson and Zora Neale Hurston, helped to bring a sense of legitimacy to the black dialect that had been so badly castigated by mainstream culture.

As significant as were the writings, art, and other foci of blacks during the Renaissance, there was no melding of them toward any characterization that could be considered as a black student movement. Harry Edwards, a premier observer of black students, writes:

> The Black student movement had its beginnings in the idealism, ingenuity, and just plain guts of young Black men and women who were attending southern Negro colleges in the late 1950's and 1960's.[4]

Although oppression and denial of civil rights were realities in the lives of black students, they were neither new nor unique to them. After all, their forefathers and foremothers, virtually all blacks who had some history in the slave experience, suffered those or similar indignities. In time an attitude called "redemptive suffering" came to the fore. Strength, character, and greater humanity were thought to reside in the suffering and oppression systematically heaped upon black people.

Soon after the opening of World War II, the threatened March on Washington, by A. Philip Randolph, and hundreds of thousands of blacks threatening to tie up the federal structure unless blacks were accorded equal opportunities in the defense industries encouraged President Roosevelt's Fair Employment Practices Committee.[5] Randolph, head of the Brotherhood of Sleeping Car Porters, did not plan to base his march on the loyalty and dedication to struggle for liberation on the college student population, nor upon the educated black category, although many of the Pullman porters were college graduates or at least college trained. His appeal was directly to the working class, especially those in the factories and critical defense industries.

The success of these defense workers was felt a decade or so later when their children were ready for college. Even though these students were by no means affluent, they were relatively more secure than any generation of black youth had been before. When they went to college, or to work directly from school, they felt the sting of segregation and discrimination and were less willing to tolerate it than their parents had been.

Because parents had suffered much and understood the imperfections of the world, as well as the price that could potentially be paid for "rocking the boat," they and the teachers of their children, counseled the collegians to find ways of holding onto their dignity by not challenging each and every evidence of discrimination that they might face. Students of the early 1950s and 1960s were not willing to play by the old rules of the game. Collegians and their parents often fell out over the issue of pushing for rights or accommodating to second class citizenship. Any deviation by students from hard study, evidenced by the acquiring of acceptable grade point averages, meant a confusion of priorities by the student. The achievement of education would assure that life would be better, even if all civil rights were not gained. The black student movement thus began with the rejection of the complacency that relative economic security provided for black parents.[6] They did not generally turn on their parents but did not take their advice to avoid confrontation with the racist social structure.

Black students, however idealistic and alienated they were, did not cohere into a group capable of fomenting a movement until the late 1950s. It could easily be thought that there was little protest activity among black people before then. It is often forgotten that there were over 200 slave rebellions before the Civil War, though those of Gabriel Prosser, Denmark Vesey, and Nat Turner are the ones most publicized.[7] Other persons protested individually, as the record shows.[8] Even after Reconstruction, when Jim Crow raised its head, individual protest was very common.[9] There was protest in testing the limits to which individuals could go in their quest for equal citizenship. Especially qualified blacks challenged authorities to allow them to further their education. The Law School Cases began in the 1930s, when Donald Murray sought to enter the Law School of the University of Maryland.[10] Lloyd Gaines petitioned to enter the University of Missouri Law School in 1936, and Hemon Sweatt applied to enter the University of Texas Law School in 1946.[11] Occasionally, an individual's protest yielded results, such as when Silas Hunt was admitted to the University of Arkansas Law School in 1948 upon the strength of his application.[12] Individual protest, though, could be seen as a forerunner to wider-scale group protest. The impetus there, of course, was the Brown decision of 1954, which served only to whet the students' appetites for greater freedom and the removal of all vestiges of segregation and lack of civil rights. Now they were willing to join in all efforts aimed at removing disabilities and affirming citizenship. Now they saw merit in the efforts of Rosa Parks to reject segregated seating on Southern buses. If a forty odd year old black woman without higher education could challenge for dignity, why not themselves, young, less encumbered, and better armed for the struggle? More importantly, they, unlike their more middle class parents, did not see a need to separate from the black masses mired in the lower classes in order to prove their acceptability to ruling whites.

South Carolina State College, where Miss Howie taught, was not very different from other black colleges, public or private. It had the usual compliment of persons—student and faculty—who were striving for status, using the campus and its activities toward that end. And like others, although it was South Carolina's only state-supported higher learning institution for blacks, it had competition from other private black colleges, such as Claflin and Vorhees. Miss Howie's initial task, as that of so many other educators, was to use the concerns of the students as building blocks for development. This meant giving especial opportunities to students who appeared to be more promising, and promoting those, sometimes at the expense of other students, who did not have perceived early promise. Getting them to stretch their imagination and thoughts beyond the campus was difficult, for the campus literally constituted their world. Governor James F. Byrnes had already set the tone against integration and the promotion of protest in South Carolina by saying publicly, regarding the Brown case:

> Should the Supreme Court decide this case against our position, we will face a serious problem. Of only one thing we can be certain, South Carolina will not now, not for some years to come, mix white and colored children in our schools.[13]

Miss Howie never accepted the suggestion or recommendation of Governor Byrnes, nor that of any other public official who stressed the separation of the races which meant a relegation of one group to a position lower than another. While every college administrator understood that government would be involved in the operation of their institution, it was clear that the top leadership of South Carolina, exemplified in the behavior and thoughts of the governor, had no intention of democratizing education in that state. There was no real way of openly fighting that orientation without risking great losses to the group Howie was trying to help. Ways had to be found by tunneling under the political opposition to equality. South Carolina State College was thought of as politically vulnerable. The constant threat from high state politicians to shut down the school, with dire consequences to the mobility aspirations of black people of the state compelled the leadership of the school to show as little militancy as possible.[14] It was a long time before teachers with activist orientations could function normally as professors by engaging the students with critical materials and interpretations. Even during the era of the sit-ins leaders at South Carolina State College had to find students from Claflin College (Orangeburg), Morris College (Sumpter) and Friendship College (Rock Hill) to support the movement.[15]

But even if the schools that black students attended were not rated among the top few in the country in prestige and status, the students understood that they were still relatively privileged compared to their friends who did not attend college. There was a growing feeling, especially during the 1960s and 1970s that their privilege would need to be offset by their working toward the improvement of the status of their own people. Leroy Clark wrote:

> There is a quickening sense of responsibility devolving upon this young group. They are struggling to define themselves and to create a modus operandi for their contributing to their community. And despite the public "excellence" and accomplishment which many display, this growing desire to use themselves in significant ways is probably confronting feelings of self-doubt and inferiority which few, if any blacks in this society can escape, no matter how favored or gifted. ....[16]

It is impossible to understand the lives of individuals without reference to the conditions in which they have lived and worked. Marguerite Rogers Howie spent most of her working life in a black higher educational context. Many stories have been told about the black institutions and their influence or impact upon the lives and futures of black youth. Their problems have been known for many years. But so pertinent are they that it is necessary again to briefly tell their story.

Black colleges and universities are thorns in the sides of the state legislatures which fail to appropriate enough funds for their improvement.

By remaining poor the black schools remain poor in influence and pro-ductivity. Legislatures assure little growth, relative to the potential of the schools, through their penurious appropriations based upon the number of students enrolled and the cost of their programs, and not upon the needs and abilities of the schools to carry out meaningful programs of teaching and research.

As state colleges historic inequities are only recently being considered. Though they have for years served as universities, their appropriations tended to be relatively smallest. Their positions, vis-à-vis other state col-leges and universities remain largely noncompetitive. This, despite the fact that some schools have started to receive more equitable appropriations.

The black colleges draw as many good students potentially as are found in any school, though sociological forces over which they have no control mask the performance of many. A large number of these students have special problems, all of which are not academic in nature.

The black university draws students from other states who want to leave their communities where they had problems, such as children out of wedlock. In Border States, it draws white students, from local areas, whose families were so large or poor that barring their going to a cheap school, education for them would be practically out of the question. It draws a large number of middle age whites who have had breaks in their training to have babies, fight wars, work, etc. Black students from the in-ner cores of our large cities come in profusion, though they are only a frac-tion of those who could profit from training. These students participated in the integration of elementary and high schools. The impersonality of teaching there, the imposition on them of learning and teaching mores foreign to them, as well as uneducated, transient faculties, meant they got little out of classes. Some good students were relegated to nonacademic tracks or even to poor trade tracks reflecting more their sociological con-ditions than their abilities to learn. After finishing high school, some felt they would have better chances to make something out of themselves if they went to a Negro school where traditionally teachers have taken up time with the students.

But even in the black university the student runs into problems. A few preliminary comments will clarify this point.

Every year, from about the first of February through about the first of August, black universities undergo a period of travail. In addition to student disturbances, one sees the senseless termination of contracts of many able teachers, white and black, who have a basic commitment to the betterment of the colleges. Many whose heads have rolled have done no more than aired for open discussion problems that have been discussed privately under breaths of fear. They have often gone beyond the call of duty in the help of students who desperately needed it. They have generated an air of excitement in the learning challenge and their balanced scholarship would be a compliment to any college.

Some instructors have been fired who had specialized knowledge and training and upon whose shoulders completely new and much needed programs were being built. Like the others, they did nothing that could be considered damaging to persons in power or to the school. Legitimate and certain very minor compromises were all they sought, all of which they felt would benefit the school and its students.

Black colleges contain basic factors conducive to discord. Their poverty is a continuing problem from which most others flow. Usually no one of high leadership has been willing to rise above selfishness and think about the college as a channel of opportunity for all qualified citizens, regardless of race or station in life. Most ranking administrators gained their training and positions at times when color barriers were legal and a part of custom. They saw opportunities and the world in terms of a struggle between black and white. They saw security in terms of power wieldable from prestigious positions. They often courted, and were courted by, persons of the opposite race who had only imaginary power and influence. This was a stratagem for their own survival. They isolated themselves from both students and faculty and seldom declared or campaigned in places of power for the growth of their schools.

Most leaders were tired, having fought racism for years, and no longer had the vitality to do battle in the politico-educational arena where tactics and strategies are forever changing and sharpening. They alienated younger faculty men and women with vigor and determination to make the colleges grow, misinterpreting their actions as grabs for power.

These leaders have done good jobs, under the circumstances, but have been unable to bring excitement and vitality and progress to their schools because of imaginary threats to their own security. Their preintegration day philosophies of education have not been subject to modification in times when change is everywhere. Public involvement in controversy, where legitimate change is sought, is interpreted by them as unfavorable publicity that is damaging to the school.

So local has the job of black college leadership become that Chamber of Commerce men are believed able to sway school policy. Top leaders are divided and suspicious of each other. They do not like to confront other leaders and go for days, sometimes weeks, without communicating directly with each other. Important decisions are sometimes handled too often by secretaries who, through time and necessity, have had to make decisions to keep the school running because of the failure of leaders to act at the right time.

There is also a tendency to overlook expertise on the faculty, even when decisions have to be made in the area where a professor holds recognized competence...

Some departmental chairmen have such little confidence in their staffs that they do not permit them to counsel majors relative to courses and will not allow them to have private offices. By threatening to or actually blocking promotions and killing or discouraging research and writing initiative within the departments, morale runs low, vitality is low, and student growth is stifled. Certain departments, though, with the blessing of the leadership and community, achieve, through vigorous leadership, growth that surpasses that of departments of equal drawing power that have been at the school for more than thirty years.

Older black administrators, taken as a group, have continued their tenures under the assumption that their schools should not depart from an elitist tradition. Prior to the 1954 decision forcing integration, the better financed state and private black colleges admitted students who were closer to middle class family status than is now the case. Perhaps a large segment of the black student population were children of parents who held the few favored positions—teachers, undertakers, postmen, doctors, and preachers—in the segregated society. Although these students were objectively poor, they were not as poor, relatively, as those who did not make it to college. Being in college was a sign of achievement or a symbol of family prosperity. In earlier days fewer programs existed to help needy college students thus leaving family affluence as the main factor in the student's battle for education.

Having been favored themselves by having received degrees from prestigious schools in the Midwest or East (and occasionally from the West), faculty men who became black college administrators soon tried to make their schools over into the images of those they attended. Although they did not succeed, some schools did gain prestige among blacks, perhaps more for singing and partying than for scholarship. ... States with several junior colleges and poor four year ones allowed the largest and best financed of the black schools to become the schools of the elite. Rockefeller and other foundation money made schools such as Morehouse, Spelman, Bennett, Fisk, and Hampton elite schools. Federal funds made Howard the most highly rated of them all. Tuskegee alone, among the noted black schools, continued to work mainly with common man students (The change of the name of Tuskegee from an Institute to a University, suggests a change of orientation by that noted institution.).

Somehow a tradition of working with common students did not develop at black colleges for many of the older staff and administrators were geared practically and psychologically for dealing with the children of the "black elite." Even today, in the face of large scale socioeconomic change, older teachers revel in a dream world, over the quality of students they used to get.[17]

7
Diversity in the Association

The 1930s were a time of heightened black awareness and the finding of more that was positive about the group. The Harlem or Negro Renaissance was no doubt the best expression of this new found faith. It was not an anti-majority period; it was not nationalistic, and majority members who were most inclined were welcomed, indeed encouraged, to find communion with the black people on a basis of equality. Some of these majority members encouraged blacks to persevere and achieve and were willing to offer them financial sponsorship, if they were able. Some of the more notable of the Harlem Renaissance writers and artists were sponsored by majority group members.

There are several reasons that there were white faculty members at many of the private black institutions at a time when Southern state laws prohibited the interaction of the races on social levels. Many black colleges were begun after the Civil War and during or shortly after Reconstruction. The Freedmen's Bureau had been the federal agency most concerned with education of the former slaves. The Bureau made funds available to many religious groups and associations willing to undertake the work of education of the freedmen. A figure of $1 per freedman has been suggested as the amount available to a congregation or association engaging in that work. In big concentrations of freedmen the funds available could become quite substantial. General Samuel Chapman Armstrong began Hampton University; General O.O. Howard began Howard University and General Clayton Fisk, commander of the military district in which Tennessee was located, was the founder of Fisk University. Although the numbers of colleges begun exceed 600, most were not of collegiate level.[1] Many were essentially elementary and secondary schools which, over time, were upgraded to collegiate status. The number of potential black faculty members was necessarily small because of such a small number of persons who had received training beyond the elementary grades. Most of the schools, public and private, which catered to black freedmen, were staffed by white teachers who spent a term or two in the schools. They have been called "Yankee School Marms," for they were liberalized, seeing themselves with a mission of humanizing and even Christianizing the freedmen.[2]

Although most of these teachers remained only a short time, there were others who became attached to their schools and to the teaching of the freedmen. They stayed on and became identified with their schools, if at a local level. One of the most notable institutions of the post-reconstruction era was Fisk, made famous by the Fisk Jubilee Singers whose conductor was white. Organizations in other black institutions less renowned than the Jubilee Singers were often supervised by whites. Robert E. Park, later eminent chairman of the department of sociology at the University of Chicago, had served as secretary to Booker T. Washington at Tuskegee. Some of these teachers were marginalized to the majority group, for one reason or another, or perhaps because they wanted to be. Still others worked at the schools because they wanted to experience a feeling of accomplishment. Missionary zeal motivated some to remain and this meant their own rejection of the material values of the world. There were very few financial rewards to be found for working in the impoverished black schools. Still other majority members found that black schools provided data bases for writing about the black experience, which may have some payoffs later. Most, it might be argued, fell victim to what later became known as the "Bohannon Trap," or the strong likelihood of finding something positive and likeable about the group with which they lived and worked.

From the very beginning of the Association of Social Science Teachers, from which grew the Association of Social and Behavioral Scientists, the possibility existed for the participation of members representing other cultures. Aside from the fact that anyone from any ethnicity could join, read papers, and participate in the activities of the group, there was the matter of the teaching force in the black colleges. Segregation in education extended formally only to public institutions, leaving the private ones whose boards gave them greater leeway, to hire persons without respect to ethnicity. The better known black private institutions, most with religious affiliations, retained majority members on their staffs long before the Brown decision of 1954. Tougaloo College, in Mississippi, Philander Smith, in Little Rock, Arkansas, Dillard and Xavier Universities, in New Orleans, Louisiana, Hampton, in Virginia, Talladega, in Alabama, Fisk University and Knoxville College, in Tennessee, and many others, had white faculty members for many years. Indeed, Howard University did not gain a black president until the 1920s, the first being Mordecia Wyatt Johnson. Charles S. Johnson, the distinguished sociologist, was the first black president of Fisk University, taking that position during the late 1930s.

Majority members were relatively indistinctive during the early life of the organization, though they did participate when the Association met at the campuses where they taught. Because so many of the white faculty members at black schools opposed the rankest form of segregation, they were generally unwilling to accompany blacks into situations where they might be embarrassed because of favorable treatment to themselves and unfavorable treatment to black members. The question of passing has been addressed by many scholars. Ordinarily, this meant that blacks who had enough majority genotype and phenotype passed, but the practice worked the other way as well. Whites who worked at black schools had a vested interest in being identified with the schools at which they taught. If they did not openly pass as black, they often created the atmosphere that they were excused from the obligations of whites if they worked at the black schools. Practically, this often meant withdrawing from majority culture and finding fulfillment in the confines of the black experience and culture.

By the 1950s, and the Civil Rights Movement, it became more acceptable for majority members to align with the blacks who were seeking greater citizenship. The testing of the reality of the citizenship of blacks in the South was undertaken by idealistic college students, from the North and the South. White faculty members began to stand up for the rights of blacks in their own communities. By the late 1960s, a most distinguished member of the Yale University faculty and administration defected to impoverished Stilman College, in Alabama, where he felt he could do some good because the students wanted an education.[3] The death of Martin Luther King, Jr., similarly encouraged greater participation of majority members in the activities which they considered as advancing the citizenship and humanity of black people.

In the Association of Social and Behavioral Scientists, the participation of white members was noticeable. Evidently, black faculty members at the schools where they taught convinced some of their colleagues that they might enjoy attending and participating in the Association. In the early 1970s, A. Stephen Stephan, former chairman of the department of sociology, and Daniel E. Ferritor, later Chancellor of the University of Arkansas, Fayetteville, attended meetings of the Association. William Helmrich, formerly an instructor at Lincoln University, Jefferson City, Missouri, Richter Moore, of Appalachian State University, and various others read papers in the Association meetings. Moore was treasurer of the Association in 1974. Richard Robbins, a biographer of Charles S. Johnson, was another majority member, from Boston University, who attended frequently. Numerous distinguished majority scholars published in the Association journal.

East Indians have been fairly well represented in the social sciences in the majority black schools. They have participated notably over the years and have written papers for the Association journal. Joghinder Dillon, of Florida A&M University, and B. Krishna Singh, of Virginia Commonwealth University, have notably represented the Indian group.

These members have engaged in the issues of the Association and in their most difficult and heated debates. They were never treated as, nor did they see themselves, as outsiders, for they felt comfortable with the Association members whom they knew.

The matters of recognition and advancement were bound to arise in the Association, and they applied to majority and other ethnic participants as well as to blacks. As in so many associations, continued participation on a year-to-year basis enhanced the likelihood of recognition. Those persons who attended for only a few years running effectively disqualified themselves for Association recognition, for neither they nor their contributions were well known.

Only a few majority members participated to the extent that they became enmeshed into the inner workings of the organization. There is no evidence that any majority member became executive secretary, editor, or associate editor of the journal, or in the pipeline for the presidency. John Griffin was the first majority member to receive the W.E.B. Du Bois Award. Most give up participation after several years. The reasons for their doing so are no doubt numerous. These persons may change their academic locations, making it more difficult to attend the Association meetings. They may become more involved in other organizations that compete for the limited financial support their schools are willing to offer and so they must make choices of which associations mean more to them and their advancement. There is also the changing constituency of the Association. At various times there is not the same attitude toward majority members as existed earlier. Younger, more strident black scholars, taking different stances, from assimilation to separation, may read papers in the Association meetings. Sometimes their readings may sound threatening to majority members who have been participating, causing these members to become uncomfortable.[4]

Because of the small numbers of majority members participating in the Association, a change of a few persons can make an enormous difference in its organization. A few voices have been raised as to the need to assure that the organization is always inclusive, but there is no attempt to offer special or preferential treatment to any Association member. When people do rise to recognition in the Association, it is generally due to the way they use their skills in negotiation, in self-presentation, and in knowledge of the issues and problems with which the Association members generally grapple.

As in so many academic organizations, the Association of Social and Behavioral Scientists has experienced an upsurge in the thrust of women. Jacquelyne Jackson was its first Executive Secretary, taking over from J. Erroll Miller in the late 1960s. Miller ran the Association as part of his fiefdom. He served for years as Professor and head of the Division of Social Sciences at Lincoln University, Jefferson City, Missouri. When Miller departed for the University of Indiana, about 1968, the way was opened for Jackson to assume Association leadership. As a very independent thinker and a prolific writer, Jackson was determined to make her influence felt. While not a feminist, she insisted on having her viewpoints evaluated on the basis of their merit and not upon her gender. A powerful and provocative speaker, Jackson could hold her own with anyone in the Association.

At the same time that Jackson was making her bid, Marguerite Howie was beginning to assert herself, using some of the same tactics as Jackson. Since Howie was older than Jackson and more senior in the field, it was political whether she would ascend to leadership over Jackson. There were serious disputes among the women, but especially between the two. Unlike the men, whose disputes were largely confined to the meetings rooms, or to the parties that went on later, those between the women became more rancorous and personal. Small differences between the women could not be resolved and sometimes disagreements carried over from one year to the next. Although Howie won the W.E.B. Du Bois Award four years after Jackson, this, no doubt, exacerbated the widening rift between the two women who were friends other than in Association work. Jackson was the second woman to win the Du Bois Award, the first being Elizabeth Duncan Koontz, a prominent official in national public education in the Carter Administration. Howie and Koontz were longtime friends. When Jackson received the award, she ended her acceptance speech with a "Goodbye" to the Association and, by 1995, had not made another appearance. After some prodding by members, she did attend the Du Bois Award Luncheon during the 1996 meetings in Greensboro, North Carolina. The Association retains a degree of diversity within its own membership, for the spectrum of opinions and life orientations is great.

8
Howie's Work in the Larger Picture

Marguerite Howie joined the faculty of South Carolina State College in 1957 at critical time in the black quest for higher education. It was just three years after the momentous Brown decision of 1954 which outlawed racial segregation in public education. Not all southern states leaders wanted to abide by the decision and began to implement various programs and strategies of evasion. Southern governors came together under the banner of States Rights, bolting the Democrat Party to form the Dixiecrats. In philosophy they represented a southern carryover of their antagonism against President Harry Truman who had challenged the "Separate but equal doctrine," called for an end to discrimination in higher education, issued an Executive Order ending desegregation in the armed forces and an end to discrimination in the federal civil service. South Carolina's Senator Strom Thurmond was the Dixiecrat Party nominee for president. Thurmond's attitude toward black education, and especially toward South Carolina State College, was not presented as a favorable one. He seemed committed to as little change in black status as possible and sought to circumvent federal government initiatives in that direction. Perhaps Thurmond's hardness was made harder by his association with Governor Orval E. Faubus, of Arkansas, who precipitated the Little Rock Crisis of 1957 by refusing the admission and protection of nine students trying to enter Little Rock Central High School, even though graduate schools of the University of Arkansas had been integrated without incident since 1948.

Mrs. Howie was a seasoned teacher by the time she took the job at South Carolina State College. Why she waited several years before moving to the college level might be explained partly by the fact that the men by that time were not as mobile. Receiving advanced degrees often meant their becoming frozen in black schools, though they could move around relatively freely depending upon what they could negotiate from particular schools. Men with terminal degrees changed institutions quite frequently trying to rise to the apex of the black higher educational system.

Schools such as Hampton, Howard, Morgan, and the Atlanta Complex,[1] seemed to be the choices preferred by the more mobile members. After the Brown decision black males began to move to the majority schools in somewhat greater frequency than black females and women began to take their places in the black schools. Part of the trend was due to the fact that black males were more represented in the ranks of the doctoral degree seekers and holders than were the females. Later on that trend was to change. As was quite common among black females, the trend seemed to encourage their becoming much more involved in the raising of families which, for most, interfered with their vigorous pursuit of advanced degrees.

Howie was about 39 years old when she moved to South Carolina State College, showing considerable maturity and experience. Within the teaching ranks, working at the college level generally was considered near the top of the job hierarchy within black society. Women were always fairly well represented in the black college teaching ranks, but they generally were not permitted to rise very high in the administrative structure, outside of those positions which had most to do with the management of women students.[2]

While movement to the college meant some personal mobility for Howie, there must have been other things that she wanted to accomplish. By 1957 the changes occurring in higher education generally meant that a new challenge faced the teachers in the black colleges. Would students be satisfied with faculty members who were not involved in change—with faculty members who valued their own security so much that they steered clear of any degree of confrontation with the defenders of the status quo? On the surface it might appear that Ms. Howie was not a likely candidate for expecting and promoting change either on her campus or in the more general community. Gender was an obvious limitation to serious involvement at that time. When women were activist it was mostly within the social arena, involving work with female students or some group of females in the college community. Women of the previous years had not directly challenged the system, even though those such as Mary McLeod Bethune, Margaret Murray Washington, Mary Church Terrell and others had been important speechmakers before Howie was born. The Harlem Renaissance women had not mounted direct challenges against the segregationist structures even though their pens were active. There had been no female counterpart to Richard Wright's Bigger Thomas. Women were expected to exhibit their disgust with the segregated system in other more acceptable ways. Women were no doubt discriminated against less harshly than black males and they found adjustment to the system in their roles as women to be less stressful. There were more ways for women to circumvent the system than for males. Ernest Gaines had tried in the

1950s to create a sense of activism in black women in the form of direct confrontation when he penned the *Autobiography of Miss Jane Pittman.* Wrapped in the symbolism of old age, Miss Pittman directly challenged the segregationist system of the South by getting herself a drink of water at a white only fountain. Gaines knew that there was some respect for age in the South and that age provided a barrier of security, excusing those who were in that status from the usual attacks against those who were young. Few old black persons were ever assaulted by even the Ku Klux Klan for they were not considered threats to the system. Had a young person done what Miss Jane Pittman did, the consequences could have been dire, at least according to the propaganda of the time. The teachings of the South were to condition blacks to maintain a certain place, generally a low one, in the society and those conditionings were aimed at the younger members.

It was most unexpected that there would be a shift from verbally attacking the system to a direct assault on it. Not much attention had been given to the influence of women even though Rosa Parks had set the stage in 1955 with her refusal to move to the back of a segregated Montgomery bus. Daisy Bates was just making her bid for national recognition as leader of the Little Rock Nine[3] when Howie moved to South Carolina State College. While women did not swing into direct action as a group, here and there they were preparing themselves for greater involvement in the struggle for human rights. Marguerite Howie found it best to engage in the struggle on the terms that she knew best, that is, through preparing the students whom she taught in her classes. This in no way meant that Mrs. Howie was even minimally satisfied with the position that black people occupied in South Carolina society.

Mrs. Howie was, in the language of dichotomist Gaye Williams,[4] a pre-integration baby. Williams, though, gave more attention to her own status as a post-integration child. Howie's intentions were, of course, quite different from those of Williams who came onto the scene a generation or more later. For most of Howie's life, before the Brown decision, there were direct structures to assault and not much time or energy left to deal with identities or ideology. The world had given her an identity and anchored it within the structure created and maintained for black people. Pre-integration children had understood that fleeing from blackness was one way of advancing in society, and even in black society. This meant developing a way of life which included as few black people as possible, and then only those of the upper middle class who adopted mobility as a religion. These pre-integration persons sought to build as high a wall as possible between themselves and other members of their group. Their plan was not much different from that of the majority group which sought to segregate itself into classes or status groups which were socially self-contained. While the higher class members drew much of their economic support from the members of their lower classes, they had very little to do with them socially.

Although there were always some blacks who were affluent, even during the darkest periods of their history, the majority were practically undifferentiated economically. The focus of "within group" differentiation had to be placed on other factors. The major differentient within black society was educational for with it individuals had access to a wider range of opportunities, especially within the professional world. The opening of schools and the ready endorsement of education as the one avenue of mobility open to talent only placed nearly all blacks on the same social footing. From that base competition began with previous status and family connections becoming less and less important. As Adolph Reed, Sr., notes, when all blacks had to sit on the back of the bus (a metaphor for suffering the entire range of legally and socially permissible discriminations) there was not all that much to separate one from the other.[5] Adjusting to that reality led some to concentrate on ephemera such as color which had value within the group but not outside it.

Pre-integration blacks had their work cut out for them. They could work toward the dismantlement of those structures which retarded their mobility simply on the basis of their phenotype (color or race) or they could retreat into the group building cocoons around themselves which softened the blows of discrimination.

When Rosa Parks acted defiantly in a quest for recognition as an ordinary citizen, she redefined the attitudes that black people had toward themselves. Now it was not necessary to prove that one was alienated from black people but it was more important to show that one was with the group and its aspiration for change. Howie had always been interested in change and now there was a much better platform from which she could advocate change, even as a college professor.

There were other changes which were affecting the way that teachers such as Marguerite Howie conducted their work. The freeing of the African countries from colonialism, beginning with Sudan in 1956, and especially with Ghana, in 1957, coincided with events such as the Montgomery Bus Boycott and the Little Rock Crisis. Black people were moving for change on a broad front. By the time of the sit-ins of the late 1950s and early 1960s students were more ready than ever to engage the system. The teachings of the past and the preparation of the students to seek mobility through black rejection and imitation of majority values lost their currency. Pre-integration teachers, administrators, and role models would have to change or be swept aside as totally irrelevant by the new breed of students who were less fearful, more strident and demanding of change. The post-integration period was in sight long before that goal was reached.

Historians and chroniclers seek out momentous events and personalities to emphasize for future generations to consider. The dominant black personality of the period from 1955 to 1968 was, without doubt, Martin Luther King, Jr. The entire history of a people and their movements for change and justice is often attempted to be told in the life of King for the name King is noted world wide. Agencies, organizations, and individuals feel almost an indebtedness to the magic of the personality of King. But the history and meaning of Nazism cannot be told in the life and psychology of Adolf Hitler. Nor can the valor and heroism of the English people enduring the blitzkriegs, blackouts, and privation be told in the stirring remarks of Prime Minister Winston Churchill. The Russian people, who suffered some 27 million killed during the Holocaust of World War II cannot have their stories told in the lives, however stirring, of Stalin and Marshall Zukhov. America reveled in the heroism of its most visible leaders Generals Dwight David Eisenhower and Douglas MacArthur nearly ignoring the exploits and bravery of thousands of privates and ordinary soldiers whose names never made even their local newspapers. In reference to the King stories, other personalities and their acts, even in support of the movement, are viewed as mere appendages to King. The further they were from King the less even their appendage status was appreciated.

Marguerite Howie was professing at South Carolina State College when King was at the top of his popularity and fame. He was, from the standpoint of the controlling Southern leaders, the most dangerous man in America. King had to be tied to an international plot to overthrow America. The only group dedicated to that cause, so the propagandists taught, were the communists, either directed by or with ties to the Soviet Union. In simple terms, King was a communist. Southern states had been the hardest on communists, even academic ones. Under the inspiration of the McCarthy Years, beginning in the early 1950s, these states had moved to declare as communists persons who even voiced alternative theses for the organization of the country. In states like Arkansas, the legislatures moved to outlaw the employment of communists in public positions. Since there were almost no other communists of national visibility in the country, the Rosenbergs having been executed by 1952 for collaborating with the Soviets in the transfer of atomic secrets, the Act 10 legislation in Arkansas, though ostensibly anticommunist was in fact anti-King.

Professors such as Howie tried to continue their work though in the shadow of the King momentum and before students who saw many contradictions between learning essentially a useless "white man's curriculum," and trying to find the means to seriously challenge the system for real change.

Until the death of King professors such as Marguerite Howie were in something of a limbo as to the direction they wanted their teaching to take. They could use the older norms of instructing the students in directions that did not have much to do with social change. It might be politically incorrect for them to push the students in a particular direction for a degree of balance had to be maintained for the state to continue to support the school. Too much activism could mean changes of presidents who were expected by the political system to maintain tight control over the students as well as over the more aggressive faculty members. Black presidents had received some signals from their political bosses, or those who thought themselves politically superior, that very dim views would be taken of their letting students get out of hand by engaging in excessive activism. Their schools were so closely tied to the political system, owing to their lack of independent budgets and endowments, they, as well as their schools, remained vulnerable. Perceptive presidents saw the instability created by the King initiatives as opportunities to press for the development of their schools. The overall goals of the schools were to become upgraded so that they would not be mainly identifiable as black schools, either through appearance or ideology. The only way this was thought able to be done was not to antagonize the persons who had most to say about the appropriations to the schools.

When King was killed, there was a redefinition of the attitude of the role of the black schools. The students were so sobered and hurt by the loss of King that many decided that traditional education did not have much value unless it taught individuals how to promote their own freedom. At various colleges, the students challenged their leaders. Riots broke out in the schools and in the cities. At some schools, black students torched major buildings and at others the faculty lost practical control. Ranking black politicians—mostly state representatives, there being very few black senators—were brought in to try to calm the students. The use of politicians in an educational environment only rankled some of the faculty members and indicated to them that they basically had no control over the students. The symbolism of the use of political power backfired and more often than not the students got even further out of hand. Political problems grew in importance and teaching became even harder to accomplish. Professors such as Marguerite Howie were in a serious bind for now they could not control the students as they had in the past. More significantly, the students lost some confidence in their teachers for not being more forceful in agitating for change in the political arenas. It was an almost impossible situation for these teachers for it was very unclear as to which direction the education of their charges should take.

It is difficult to fully understand a person's work in a discipline without giving some attention to the formation of that discipline. Again, it is necessary to return to a brief history of the discipline of sociology in order to see how Professor Howie's options were constrained by its founding and its operation.[6]

Howie's Working in Sociology: A Colonial Discipline

Sociology was born during the period of colonialism, a period when most of the underdeveloped or nonwestern world was either threatened with or under the actual domination of other powers. The nations of Europe were belligerent, disorganized, and seeking to take each other over. They were engaged in almost constant military struggle. The Hanseatic League had been seeking to organize the business interests that prevailed in what became Germany. Relationships with the rest of the European powers were not amiable. The Holy Roman Empire had been more of an economic operation than one interested in the saving of souls. Even Martin Luther's revolt against the Catholic Church, in the early 1500s, showed the disorganization and conflict that existed in those religious ranks. In a real sense, there had been attempts by the Church to subjugate those who were not believers or supporters in the classic colonial process. France, England, Spain, and Portugal had engaged upon colonialism in the acquiring of territories in the New World subjugating whole populations of people in the process. Germany would engage in the sweepstakes as soon as it was strengthened by unification under the chancellorship of Otto von Bismarck. Italy understood its vulnerability and had to engage upon its own colonization program. In the Orient colonization by the European powers was eminent. India, made up of a large number of principalities, and fragmented by caste, linguistic, religious, and class division, was one of the earliest of the territories to fall under control by the European powers, especially Great Britain. Japan, Russia, and China were also feeling vulnerable. Colonialism was the political idea that sought to sweep the world, and those groups that were too weak to resist were defined as socially expendable.

Darwinism arose in the midst of this turmoil, not so much because it was a plausible doctrine or theory, but more likely because it was a set of eyeglasses out of which the theorists had to see the world.[7] It has been known for a long time that people see the world from the positions in which they find themselves. John Ray (1627-1705), a British clergyman, naturalist, and a founder of systematic natural theory, was unable to see the world except out of the eyes of a man of the cloth, a man of God, a preacher.[8] Darwin was a man of learning who had enough social status to allow him to take a trip around the world observing the flora and fauna in places that were under control of the English. Because there was such hostility between the colonizing powers, it is unlikely that they would have permitted a British ship to freely visit their ports and scientists from those ships to conduct their observations unimpeded. Even though Darwin claimed not to be much interested in human conditions in the places where he observed, there is every likelihood that he was not blind to those conditions. Even if he did not say so, he no doubt interpreted the conditions of colonized people within the framework of the "struggle for survival," the concept which, in the social sciences, became known as Social Darwinism.

The conditions in which men found themselves, and in which they were socialized, formed the foundation from which they envisioned the world. That foundation was, for all but the most daring, almost the limiting reality. Whatever a person thought, or believed, was merely a reflection of the environment in which he was formed. The serf was not likely to think outside that category. The nobleman could not easily transcend his position. Nor could the academic easily escape the teachings handed down by the "grand masters" of their disciplines.

Marxism also arose within the context of colonialism. Like the Social Darwinists, who came afterwards, Marx was restricted to seeing the world from the position in which he was socialized. The conflict between the rich and poor, between the haves and have-nots, between the bourgeoisie and the proletariat, he thought, was as old as the struggle for survival in the natural order. The outcome would be the same. Marx suggested revolution as the only way to redress the maldistribution of wealth between the rich and the poor and the institution of socialism or communism. His claim was for the destruction of the very concept of private property and replacing it with the notion of collective ownership of property relevant to human prosperity and comfort.

It is not necessary herewith to review the voluminous writings on this idea. Instead, our intention is to show the great difficulty of seeing and interpreting out of the context in which one has been socialized. The framers of the discipline of sociology were all steeped within the colonialist context. There is little evidence that these men had any other framework from which to draw their conclusions. Comte, a founder of the discipline, could only think of the stability of society occurring within a colonialist framework. He did not write much about the colonialism of the French, at home or in the New World. He was less concerned, for instance, with the American and Haitian Revolutions, both expressions against colonialism, than he was with what was happening to his beloved France.

Herbert Spencer, the English scholar, and a founder of the discipline, was as ensteeped in colonialist thought as those around him. His idea of the natural ranking of people grew out of his long years of socialization within a colonialist framework. From where he sat, and from whence he observed, it was forthcoming that he would see the world from that position. Spencer's looking at society, local and worldwide, was like looking through a keyhole. What he saw took on the form of the keyhole. Weber, Durkheim, Sumner, and other earlier discipline founders faced the same problem, namely that of seeing and interpreting out of their socialization and experience.

Colonialism conditioned their notions of the structure of society just as surely as the thought of Aristotle conditioned the notions of science for the Western world until he was overthrown during the late Renaissance. Colonialism went on so long that whole generations of people were socialized in it and came to believe that it was the natural condition of mankind, that is, to be either members of the ruling classes or members of the subordinate groups. Each would seek to cast its thought in what they called a "realistic framework." "That is the way things are," is the reasoning of the realist. In sociology realism is thought of as what is happening here and now in the world outside the ivy-covered groves of academe.

Colonialism survived for some 400 years in various places of the world. It is not completely dead today, but everywhere it is forced to beat retreat. The conditions for its existence have disappeared and along with it the very logic that supported it for so long. Colonialism did not die because someone felt that it was immoral to hold other people in bondage and subjugation. It died because it was no longer efficient enough to prove its viability. Proof of its lack of promise lay in the numerous problems the colonialists faced, among and between themselves, and with the very people the system sought to suppress. It utilized every logic possible, including natural science, to try to make a claim as to the plausibility of colonialism and the unequal structuring of opportunity for prosperity.

Sociology is a colonialist invention, in the sense that it emerged as a way of thought during the period of colonialism. It thereby reflected the chief concerns of the controllers of the colonialist enterprise. Since it was a tool of the colonialists, its natural use would be for the furtherance of that class or for the subjugation of those colonized. Its invention was much like Eli Whitney's invention of the cotton gin. It would be beneficial to the landowners and disbeneficial to the slaves because it would promote a raising of cotton at the lowest price possible. When colonialism was overthrown sociology would no longer have a basis of support and would have to redirect its efforts or drop out as a discipline in the same processes it had largely predicted for those at the bottom of the social structures it had observed for more than 100 years.

The founders of the discipline of sociology had postured the field as dedicated to an objective study of society. The claim was that utilizing objectivity in the procedures of study would place the discipline on a scientific footing. On that footing could be made any statements that seemed to have such a grounding. The findings were always interpretational and seldom were they conclusions that were not already ensconced in tradition or supported by those with colonialists' motivations. The colonizer views himself as having more privileges than any of the colonialized. In a colonial discipline, any sociologist thought his or her interpretations to be superior, or more privileged, than that of any of the colonized—the ones studied.[9] Thus, proving that colonized people, under whatever names they went, when done objectively, had the same effect as if the conclusions were reached sentimentally. In colonialist science, everyone already knew the outcome of any study of human groups. The study would inevitably support the existing inequalities between the colonialists and the colonized.

9
Common Paradoxes

We all live lives of paradox and conflict and so it was with Marguerite Howie. One of the paradoxes in her life was that of trying to strike and maintain a balance between the requirements of being a beautiful and talented young girl turning into womanhood, expecting all the emoluments of that status, and the realities which presented themselves. It was paradoxical that one so gifted had so much trouble reaching the goals ordinarily within her grasp. To the outside world, it appeared that those with the best endowments had the best opportunities. That conclusion could be based on the Horatio Alger myth. In that myth it is possible that anyone may rise to wealth, fame, and fortune by exercise of talent, hard work, and opportunity. It is a convenient myth which, though belied by the data and evidence, remains within the thoughts of the public. There are enough examples available at any time offering enough reinforcement to convince people of the correctness or truth of the myth. In our own times women such as Jacqueline Kennedy Onassis, a very beautiful and talented woman, married John F. Kennedy, scion of the socially prominent Kennedy family, and eventually became America's First Lady as the wife of President John F. Kennedy. The idea prevailed that Jackie Kennedy had the right ingredients to practically destine her for success and recognition. Such cases are few but they are sufficient to offer the idea that given those qualities success is practically assured. Greatly talented women, even those who have enjoyed public adulation, on the other hand, have not always enjoyed almost automatic success.

Finding a true and fulfilling role for a woman was easier said than accomplished. If she became educated, her options were not enlarged, but were diminished for there was an expectation that educated people make most of their important social contacts with other educated people. But there were not that many educated males around who would consider her or who would be considered by her. The paradox of the educated black woman has been known for many years and some mothers counseled their daughters to get the MRS. before they got their Ph.Ds.

Marguerite Howie's case is merely illustrative of the paradox that almost any educated or accomplished woman faces within America, or perhaps in other countries as well. With talent and opportunity will she set out to conquer the world, to break new ground, to make a mark independent of her already ascribed status set largely by gender and race? Or will she settle for what society has generally expected of her—really more modest achievements within the already set parameters. Some women perceive of the paradox early and began to deal with it as others have done before. The role laid out for these women is clear and understandable. By a certain age a young woman will complete her formal schooling, look for a mate, secure a job, at least for a time, then begin to raise a family in the timeless cycle engaged in by the majority of women throughout the country. A number of obstacles are placed—social markers—to suggest that the person is on the proper track. Getting out of the cycle is much like getting off a well-marked and well-traveled road. Off the highway the number of unpredictable events increases.

Getting out of the cycle could cause problems. The women remaining out of it too long could be redefined as problematic. Putting off entering the role and then entering it later only means that they are much older when they begin the cycle. It then appears that the older woman with a young family is out of cycle. It may be more difficult to explain the lateness of their entry into the cycle. Some women decide they do not need to explain their actions and judiciously steer clear of those individuals and group members who are likely to inquire into their social activity.

Howie had to decide how she would negotiate the choices which faced her. If she decided to marry, there would be the problem of an acceptable partner. There may not be all that many acceptable and available options for the woman who was educated, talented, and attractive. Men, especially men of her own ethnicity, with the necessary requirements, were not very numerous. Thinking that she was especially endowed and enjoying a variety of choices, the well-endowed woman may remain single for much longer than the less educated woman while she seeks to resolve the problem of choice. Like other women, if she waited too long what were at first considered assets may turn into liabilities further restricting the choices open to her.

In 1939 when Marguerite Howie completed college the most likely option for an educated black person was to enter some level of the educational field. Classroom teaching beckoned and the call was heeded by perhaps the majority of blacks who could not find government employment or placement with large private firms. It was more difficult for the larger firms to ignore the social pressures to support equal opportunity in employment. Because of a segregated society, educated blacks had to compete most severely with other blacks and did not have to face the specter of competition from majority group members. A function of the rules of segregation was to remove the groups as mutual competitors for desirable positions. Uplift of black society became the virtual preserve of members of the black middle class, of which Marguerite Howie was a bonafide member. If an individual could find solace and fulfillment in the niche within the box of ethnicity, the educated black male or female could live a fairly comfortable and respectable life within the group.

As Mrs. Howie found, 1939 was not a good time for a black woman to emerge from college with a degree. The land was writhing in the last phases of the Great Depression. There was no relief in sight although some war spending had begun to supply the British against the legions of Adolf Hitler and in support of the Chinese of Chiang Kai Shek against the Japanese. Teacher salaries were as low as $30 dollars per month in some districts, and even lower for those who did not have degrees. The tendency, then, was to give the jobs to teachers without degrees, or to require no degrees at all, largely as a price-cutting scheme, for the quality education of blacks was not a major priority. This tendency, of course, encouraged many youth to drop out of college for to remain and receive a degree could lower chances for getting a job. Mrs. Howie's option, not unlike that faced by countless others, was to prolong the uncertainty by acquiring additional training and degrees against the possibility the system would open up whereupon remunerative employment might be found.

Although World War II broke out for the Americans on December 7, 1941, there was no immediate and discernible change in the lives and opportunities of black people for some time to come. President Roosevelt's claim to erase discrimination in jobs in federal employment and in the defense industry had the effect of drawing black workers from the farms of the South to the ghettos of the North where concentration became more noticeable. If anything, the schools and services became more segregated because the housing market was not desegregated until restrictive covenants were declared unconstitutional in the early 1960s in Shelly v. Kramer. They were not enforced until well into the 1970s.

Marguerite Howie could follow the legions of black people to the North, with the likelihood of being literally swallowed up as efforts were made to retrain the many Southern blacks into the requirements of Northern living, or she could remain in the South where the values and standards were more clearly defined. In exchange for some security she would forego opportunities to achieve greater financial standing as well as recognition in a wider environment. She decided that her task lay in the South with the opportunities and disadvantages provided there.

Whether in the North or the South, the typically educated black person, male or female, was ambiguously placed. There was the continuing need for group uplift in either location, but a deficit of mechanisms for bringing it about. The symbols of recognition for that work were very few in the circumscribed black community of the South and in the increasingly disorganized ghettos of the North. It was more tempting to abandon the struggle in either environment and strike out for personal gain and improved lifestyles as evidenced in increased material accumulation and consumption.

During the years of World War II, the public schools of the South provided the best way of holding onto the black youth upon whom "group uplift" in the future largely depended. Teachers needed to remain in place simply as a stratagem for encouraging the youth to put faith in themselves and in the future. Already, many of them were abandoning the schools to earn the hard cash neither they nor their parents had ever seen. Those who were old enough were able to find menial jobs largely in the households or firms of majority members whose work was needed and more handsomely remunerated in the war industries. Now more whites could afford household help; more money was flowing into the black neighborhood.

With very little to spend money for, because of rationing, those who accumulated a little had few choices. They were vulnerable to sharpies and shysters who lay in wait to provide them expensive services and trinkets. They could save for the future, or they could spend now, knowing that the future was indeed unassured. Since savings were more secure in the banks and post offices, and these positions were controlled by majority members, the black person who accumulated a substantial saving was likely to be jeopardized by those who did not wish to see the group make any forward progress. Savings were more likely to be kept at home, buried in coffee cans, secreted in dresser drawers, where they were susceptible to fire and theft. Importantly, no interest was drawing on those uninvested funds. A number of Southern black families were disorganized after the war when soldiers who had arranged for allotments to their parents or relatives returned home to find that their allotments had not been properly husbanded. Having a saving account was as much a sign of "uppityness" as was failure to observe the code of "southern etiquette."[1]

In the South, black success would still be defined within the confines of the largely segregated black neighborhood, an option that did not sit well with many who felt the war was a good time to vacate the South. Because of very sharp differentials in pay, it would be difficult for blacks to save enough money to materially alter their conditions after the war, for inflation would take its toll on any savings account. The Southern blacks would, therefore, have kept or even diminished in their economic position relative to whites.

Soon after the atomic bombs were dropped in August, 1945, bringing an end to World War II, the soldiers began to drift back home. Some sought their old menial jobs or others only slightly better. Very few returned to the plantations, which had held them and their parents for many years. The funds the soldiers received were really for their welfare, although they were called readjustment funds falling generally under the G.I. Bill. A former soldier could draw some $20 per week for a period of six months, while he looked for work. It was raised to $26 per week during the Korean War. Soldiers looked forward, optimistically, to the 26 x 26 readjustment period. A veteran could receive an allotment for attending approved classes which, hopefully, prepared him for remunerative employment. He could purchase a home, if he had the wherewithal to make the monthly mortgage payments, which most did not have; and he could receive some medical care in a veterans hospital, if his ailment were service connected and his income low enough. A limit of seven years was placed on the availability of these funds for within that time, it was hoped that most former soldiers would have readjusted upward or downward. In any case, they would have found more permanent niches and would no longer require heavy governmental support.

Since education had been the avenue which most blacks had seen as their best route to prosperity, the late war generated significant growth in black school enrollments. Persons such as Marguerite Howie could not find employment in some form of educational work with veterans or their dependents. The numerous other dislocations after the war caused by the continued vacation of blacks from the plantations caused new problems in the cities and small towns. There was something of an unwillingness, even in the South, to subject so many former soldiers to the prison system when it was known that they had rendered credible service in the defense of their country. The country had not yet slipped into post-war depression for there was still considerable spending for military uses several years after the war. It was more feasible to expand the welfare system so that the problems of the dislocation of people could be handled by social workers. For a time social work appeared to be a field in which blacks with training could find employment. Marguerite Howie was prepared for that option, having received a degree in sociology from Atlanta University.

It was, thus, within the problems confronted by blacks that Marguerite Howie confronted the paradox of employment. Had there been no black problems, there would have been no opportunity for herself, or perhaps for any other black person to find a job. Only the most disciplined and most ingenious could make a living outside of the providing of services to the problematic of the black community. The service-providers were increasingly professionalized so that credentials were more often required to provide any service to the people. As the Middle Age Enclosure Acts enabled the European upper classes to fence up property, thereby causing thousands of people to turn to pauperism and beggary, credentializing had a similar effect upon the black population in America. For any job more and more credentials were needed to compete. In public school teaching, for instance, any funds accumulated during the year from teaching salaries had to be spent during the summer for the purpose of retraining. Medical doctors, dentists, lawyers, and nearly all professionals, had to continually retrain. Private enterprise persons and entertainers were exempt from this process, though more and more memberships were required for participation. To make the situation appear to be something other than what it was, the requirement was applied to local, state, and federal government workers as well, including the military. The cost of retraining had to be recaptured through payments received for service, resulting in the providing of services for increasingly fewer people. In the black communities of the South, and in the ghettos of the North, services became even fewer and less efficient than before. More people were thrown into the streets seeking to solve their problems in the best and least economical ways possible. Even public school teachers became more isolated from the people they would serve.

College teachers, now facing the problem of furthering their training, if they did not have terminal degrees, like the public school teachers, and other public servants, were forced to continue pushing toward final degrees which by no means were assured. By the early 1950s, when black colleges were pressured to become accredited, as the teachers were required to become certified, there was a great reluctance by the authorities to award tenure to persons who did not have terminal degrees, although those without them were not often formally dismissed. Persons who were "grandfathered in" could remain on the job, but they were often pushed out at their first eligibility for retirement. Few who were young could withstand the pressure to gain full standing within their fields and disciplines, and they drifted on. Again, persons such as Marguerite Howie were forced to decide whether they wanted to help the group or to help themselves, for it was becoming more difficult to do both. They had to push on leaving little time or energy for the hard work of advocating and pressing for group advancement.

Higher education for blacks, at the time that Marguerite Howie entered it as a vocation, did not mean what it meant for members of the larger society. The smaller and more isolated the colleges, the less they were meaningfully connected to the choices being made affecting higher education. From the very beginning of higher education in America, decisions were made mainly by those who controlled the institutions. When religious groups controlled the colleges, their choices were reflected in the curricula and offerings of the institutions. The creation of a classical Christian conscience was the intent of collegiate level institutions in America from the founding of Harvard in 1636 until around the late 1700s when men like Thomas Jefferson began to challenge the utility of that kind of schooling. It was Dr. Benjamin Rush, the eminent teacher and physician who argued that the old school emphasis needed to be changed to stress the more practical. The hold of the old school foundations so resisted change that Rush advocated a federal university that would be much freer to make curriculum innovations that had more to do with practical living.

After the Civil War the formal education of blacks became problematic. Although many schools were begun that stressed a classical curriculum, it was Booker T. Washington's vision of Tuskegee, which so captivated the imagination that it became the model of black education for some time after the 1880s. Washington and Du Bois entered into vitriolic debate about the direction that black education should take—Washington stressing the practical and Du Bois the more classical. That debate continued until around 1915, until the death of Washington, but the issue was not settled. The black colleges which were designated land-grant institutions continued to mirror the joint influence of Washington and Du Bois in the curricula they offered.

It was impossible for black educators to solve the problem because they, in general, were not funding the schools. In most cases, even for the private schools, they had little control over the boards. Many of these more than 600 black colleges that were begun had benevolence as their foundation. States that began black colleges had done so mainly as a means of adhering to the minimum requirements of the law. There was never much intention of having black people receive a competitive education. If they did it was because of their own initiative or due to untiring efforts of their teachers. These colleges were not looked to as sources of knowledge, though in some cases, such as that of George Washington Carver at Tuskegee, brilliance and ability to contribute could not be overlooked. But not all of the faculty, even at Tuskegee, were as connected to the outside world as was Carver, for their contributions were considerably less notable. Teaching at the black college was more like teaching in another world. This statement was just as true at the largest and most prestigious of the black institutions as at the smaller less well-known ones. The focus was not much on answering the hard questions in natural science, the arts, or the social sciences. The real emphasis was upon social life so bitterly described by the sociologist E.F. Frazier in his *Black Bourgeoisie*. If anything, one could literally escape altogether from academic productivity and quality teaching at these institutions, if one had a mind to do so, for there were very few means for compelling adherence to the norms of quality teaching or research. The teachers were personalities more than scholars, although small numbers of them at these colleges did what they could to promote scholarship and the life of the mind. To do the latter one had to be driven more by internal than by external controls. There were enormous temptations and incentives to follow the lines of least resistance in teaching and to claim heavy teaching schedules and overwork made it impossible to do research and writing. The flight from public and serious scholarship by faculty members meant that the black college was stamped as a place where teachers were more concerned with the social than with total academic life. Consequently, few scholars at these schools reached the role of truly creative professors, although many carried the formal title.

By observation of many in the role, Howie saw the paradox of being designated a professor while not producing as one. She was determined not to fall into that trap. Although there were few incentives promoting productivity, she chose to become involved on the mental as well as the physical levels of the professorial role. She wanted to do research and writing and commenting on the problems with which social scientists deal. As soon as was feasible, she got her designation changed to the area of rural sociology, with the department of agriculture at South Carolina State. As part of a cooperative research program involving several schools, she was able to address some of the problems that were faced by rural people as they tried to make the transition to urban living. Her studies were generally state or federally funded. She wanted, however, to meet and address problems that were not within the funding purview of her supporters.

10
Sentimental Sociology

The case of Marguerite Howie also raises the question of the purpose of a social science education. Is it simply for employment, or for adducing clarifications that may be used for societal change—improvement? As very few persons are able to ignore social reality, Howie was also so constrained. If economic security were the driving concern in the application of her education, there would be little enthusiasm left for producing the research or influencing the thought that would lead to positive change. Negotiating this dilemma was a serious undertaking for Howie as it was for other persons so situated. Most likely few of them went into a field of social science with a definite idea in mind of what they wanted to do with it. The record was clear, however, that use of such training automatically in a special way, was not forthcoming. At that time it was not necessary to be certified in any of the social sciences and so holders of all degrees, and with any degree of training, could compete for nearly all of the teaching and social work jobs. Very seldom was any examination required and so candidates competed for positions on the basis of whatever political influence they could muster. The old admonition that it was not what you knew but who you knew that was most important in your getting a position, still had force. It was important to know important people, to be connected to them in the right way, to know someone who could mention one's name.

Remaining on the job was based on the same criteria as securing the job. It was still a matter of whom one knew much more than how productive one was as a scholar. Even in the field of education, at the public school level, a teacher who knew a superintendent, or whose people had worked for some board member, stood a better chance of being retained than one who did not have those connections. At the higher level, a teacher who knew a college board member could counter the influence of the president. Such teachers could remain at the institution even though they did not get along with the president or members of the administration.

The attitude was mainly a feudal one in which the peasant depended upon the attitude of the lord of the manor for mobility, or at least upon someone who had the ear of the lord. Although this attitude has often been thought of as peculiar to black schools, they were common to nearly all schools, institutions and work situations wherein the worker had to please the person highest up more than anything else. In teaching, when Marguerite Howie began, and for long years thereafter, the teacher evaluations meant a lot less than the personal relationship the faculty member had with the highest supervisor. When colleges were getting started in America, they did so on the model of the church parish, but later took on the character of an industrial plant where the faculty are employees, the trustees employers, and the president the plant superintendent.[1] Many a president of a school has been called a tyrant, an autocrat, a feudal lord.[2] College administrators are, of course, some of the most uncritiqued persons by those who work for them, and for understandable reasons. As a category, we know very little about them.[3]

The sociology of the black scholars of the first generation sharply paralleled that of the first generation of majority scholars in the sense that they were concerned with the same problems that had been defined by the majority scholars. Those concepts had most to do with issues of stratification. The earlier sociologists of the majority group had been greatly impressed by the thoughts of such men as Comte, Durkheim, and Charles Darwin. They thought that much social behavior had a basis in the socially constructed concept of race. They came perilously close to believing in a racial construction of reality. When black scholars made their entry into the field, by the time of the opening of the Harlem Renaissance, shortly after World War 1, they began to argue against biology as a cause of human conduct. The majority sociologists had the buttress of collective millions of dollars of funded research to support their claims while black scholars were denied practically any funds to conduct their research. They had to argue on the bases of data softer than those adduced by the majority scholars. When the World War 1 studies of soldiers were made public and blacks scored lower in most parts of the country, the biologists and geneticists claimed the differences were innate.[4] These scholars neither originated nor added substantially to the belief in inherited group abilities. The black social scientists had held to the idea that social behavior could only be explained on the basis of learning. They did not have the empirical data to prove their case but their argument could not be overlooked.

Majority social scientists backed down from their positions on genetically determined social behavior and in its place they substituted a concept that had almost the strength of genetics. That was the idea of caste that was attempted to be tied to genetics in the sense that it seemed so permanent. Some of the most important black scholars felt better with blacks as a caste than they did with the biological and genetic explanations. A small group of scholars, loosely organized around the thought of Oliver C. Cox, became critical of the concept of caste, but did so mostly at their schools, and then almost never in print. Cox was openly critical of the concept and no doubt paid the price in terms of social and professional mobility for doing so.[5]

The absence of funded, highly recognized rebuttal to the heavily funded research supporting caste, promoted the idea that black sociology was sentimental and therefore unworthy of being taken seriously at a time when hard, empirical data were being produced and used to support various social positions.

Within the social scientist group, the women were even less likely to engage in hard, empirical research. Their work was even more sentimental than that of the black male social scientists and, therefore, to be taken even more lightly than that of the most empirically driven of the male sociologists. Without funding for the securing of data, the black social scientists were left to counter statements made by majority group scholars which were damaging to black mobility by verbal means only. In their classrooms, they might summarily reject the findings of major scholars, holding that these scholars did not understand the black experience. Their students might also ignore these majority findings while at black schools, but they would have to internalize them when they went for further study at the majority schools. Marguerite Howie was well within the tradition of the "sentimental social scientists," even though she tried to imbue her students with the idea that they must buttress their observations and statements with empirical data. Like so many other black scholars, she had to teach from the standpoint of her own life experiences.[6]

Unless there were greater equity in the publishing of data on the black experience, minority students were under some pressure to adopt the teachings of the majority group whose teachings were directly opposed to their experience, and eventually to their mobility. Majority scholars were not likely to accept criticism of their work and so they tended to deny publication to any work that was critical of the canonized way of thinking. Only a few options were open to the black scholars. They could open their own journals and publishing houses, which few did. At some of the schools that were less threatened, or where scholars felt more secure, journals were opened. Appealing to the national black constituency, as well as to the majority, schools such as Atlanta and Howard could open such publications as Phylon: *The Journal of Race and Culture*, *The Journal of Negro History*, and *The Journal of Negro Education*. The National Association for the Advancement of Colored People *Crisis* produced valuable commentary on the black problem. Small black publishing houses struggled to bring out works by black scholars. Since these works were not from distinguished presses, they tended to be ignored by scholars of the mainstream.

11
Deviance or Conformity

Sociologists have a long history of studying individuals and groups that broke the values and expectations of society. Deviance has been viewed as a staple study by members of the discipline. The fascination with deviance has overshadowed that of conformity. Although conformists represent a much larger fraction of any population or group, the small percentage of deviants attract much more attention. It is not that the individual who is different is inherently more interesting, but the mental set that is brought to the study seems to prepare us for the study of deviance. For a profession that is most concerned with norms, it is strange that it would spend its resources so disproportionately upon a study of deviance. There is probably no course in the traditional sociology curriculum that is entitled conformity in the sense that there are courses entitled deviance. This tendency can probably only be explained in terms of the socialization of the sociologists themselves. Their mentors stressed deviance as the normal source or subject of study while conformity was downgraded. It is almost as though more can be learned about the deviant that can be applied to the conforming than if the conforming were studied.

Even that which has been considered ordinary has been turned into deviance. The housewife who cheerfully went about her duties in the 1950s by the 1980s was thought of as deviant. She is viewed as one who does not understand the nature of her exploitation within the capitalistic system.[1] Angela Davis noted a trip she took to the Masai lands in East Africa. There she saw women carrying large boards on their heads that were for the building of houses. The women did domestic work, including the building of houses. The men were cattle tenders.[2] Miss Davis did not conclude that the Masai women were being exploited because they were not under capitalism, but that women in the western world who do housework are exploited. The fact may be that there was less a tendency to see women in the underdeveloped world as exploited for only in the developed world of capitalism may sex be an exploitable commodity.

The observation of Miss Davis is significant for understanding the role of Marguerite Howie, a woman who was born some 26 years before Miss Davis and socialized during a period of capitalist exploitation of the labor of women. The rhetoric of the exploitation of females as housewives and household workers had scarcely begun. If Miss Howie conformed to the norms of that exploitation, she would be seen as not understanding that she was exploited. If she objected she would be considered as a deviant. But Marguerite Howie was not a deviant. Nor was she a conformist in the literal sense of the word. She did not diminish herself in order to make herself acceptable to the capitalist exploiters. Nor did she object to all that came her way because it was given by capitalists bent on co-opting her so that she, and people such as herself, could be more thoroughly exploited. If she promoted convention it was because she found greater rewards in conformity than she did in deviance. If she studied deviance, her plan was to see how its understanding promoted conformity. Her subjects were persons who were not allowed to conform, but who had to exhibit considerable deviance as a program for achieving conformity.

A serious problem with sociology, as seen in the case of Marguerite Howie, is that of writing and thinking in terms of rigid categories. Howie was trained in the traditional sociology of the time, a sociology of categories, in a sociology of male domination. Black male domination was simply a facet of the whole pattern of male domination, when viewed from the perspective of those who utilize the catechism of domination to address each and every social problem. One is a conformist or a deviant; an exploiter or the exploited, according to the prevailing logic of the discipline. By saying that one is conformist on some issues and deviant on others is not wholly satisfactory for all that is said in that stance is that we do not know what an individual will do. In other words, there is not much predictive accuracy about social or individual behavior.

In this work on Marguerite Howie, we have ranged over much of the history of sociology as a discipline, while trying to identify essential highlights in her life and experience. Especial attention has been given to Howie's attempt to find a place for herself within the parameters that were considered important in defining her existence. There were social forces at work over which Howie had no control and there were activities over which she had some control and with regard to which she could make choices. It has been difficult to avoid falling into the trap of defining and explaining Howie within the context of a few parameters, such as her original social class status, her status as a mixed-blood person, and her attempt to deal with her ambiguity and expected marginality. We maintain that these approaches are simply part of the conceptual and intellectual tools that have been used for analysis. They are historical, but not necessarily sharper or more appropriate than some others.

Marguerite Howie is a female sociologist of the second generation.[3] In a very strict sense, she might be called a first generation African American female sociologist. There were no outstanding female sociologists before her, that is, persons who made their living primarily in teaching and researching sociological topics. Even at the noted universities, the discipline was completely dominated by men. At majority institutions, women such as Helen Lynd[4] and Mary R. Gardner[5] were more or less afterthoughts in their departments. There were no women of sociological distinction at any of the mainstream schools until well into the 1960s. Black women before Marguerite Howie, such as Carolyn Bond Day, were peripheral to the discipline, at the schools where they taught and there were few means of fighting for centrality. Women like Ida Bellegarde, at Arkansas AM&N College,[6] and Irene Diggs, at Morgan State, were somewhat productive but were practically overshadowed by the males in their departments. Howard University did not employ a highly promising African American woman sociologist until the late 1960s with the advent of Jacquelyne Jackson and, later, Joyce Ladner.

It would be easy enough to see Howie as an anomaly, because what she was doing was different from the activities of the vast majority of other women. She was a college professor at a time when other women were afraid to test their abilities to that extent. Although women had been working for quite some time, they were mostly in the domestic fields. Yet, Howie could be seen as a woman who could not fit easily into the role set aside for her as a housewife and mother. According to Marxist sociology, these roles were dehumanizing and exploitative in the classic capitalistic pattern.

What have we learned about Marguerite Howie, a female sociologist of the second generation? It has been necessary to set her within a social and historical context, talking about the circumstances in which she grew, matured, and worked. This was done because the person cannot be separated from the social conditions. In telling the story of Marguerite Howie, we feel we have added a little bit more to the edifice of knowledge about how individuals and groups of people negotiate their social environments. Some of these persons, such as Marguerite Howie's life and work demonstrate, are more typical than we might believe.

Marguerite Howie was the kind of sociologist demanded at the time of her participation and in the situation in which she found herself. The positions she held were determined politically, and not on the basis of objective qualifications of incumbents. Mrs. Howie would no doubt say that a unique list of circumstances determined her entry into college teaching, in the first place.

The Brown decision was probably the generator of much change in the educational systems, in Southern America especially. After that decision, not even South Carolina could delay the changes that it wrought. Openings were created in many institutions, no doubt causing a siphoning off of the more mobile black faculty members to schools of higher rank within the black orbit or to majority schools that felt the pressure to modify. For example, when John Hope Franklin left Howard University for Brooklyn College, in the late 1950s, his slot had to be filled. The author filled the opening created by the departure to Atlanta University of distinguished sociologist Tilman C. Cothran, in 1959, when the effects of the Brown decision caused educational rearrangements in Arkansas. Most likely, when vacancies opened they were filled with the most promising black scholars available, generally from other black schools, including secondary schools. Sometimes the colleges were very desperate for scholars with relevant credentials. They were trying to secure or maintain their accreditation; their enrollments were growing; their resources fewer, relative to their needs. The schools saw opportunities to expand, capitalizing upon the fears of some majority schools to encounter integration for the first time in recent history.

The deeper into the South the more difficult the problem of integration. Majority Southern schools participated in every strategy possible to forestall the effects of the Brown decision. They would greatly upgrade the black schools, asking some of them to open graduate programs in order to keep black students off their campuses. Others, such as Ole Miss and the University of Alabama, would use physical means to discourage the enrollment of blacks. They would eventually require the use of Federal troops to enforce the protection of the rights of blacks to enroll. However Howie found her way into college teaching, in a sociology department, it was not because of a recognized need for expertise in that discipline. Any position was filled out of needs unrelated to those for competent performance in that discipline. Appointments depended upon how well an individual could negotiate the political system of which the institution was a part.

Had Howie wanted to become a highly productive scholar, she would have to find strength within herself, for there were practically no demands or rewards for this kind of work in the types of schools in which she taught. Not even tenure assured that a scholar was free to conduct thought and research as was more freely done in the more mainstream schools. It would, therefore, be improper to evaluate a scholar on academic productivity and contribution to disciplinary understanding when that was not why that scholar was hired, nor what she (in the case Marguerite Howie) was expected to do as her tenure progressed.

Howie's example shows that there was no complete separation of academic and social life. Her role was to teach students who would be able to go into the world and make a living, if not make names for themselves. The creation of knowledge for its own sake, or for that of the discipline she represented, was unexpected. It was a foreign norm, but one she tried to maintain in the very difficult conditions in which she taught.

If Howie did not amass an impressive vita sheet, she performed an important supplemental function. She bridged the gap between young faculty members who had been trained in totally black institutions and those who were trained in totally majority ones. Often the two groups could not easily communicate. She knew that students, in schools of whatever ethnicity was dominant where they received their training, would be judged by criteria different from those which she confronted. They would have to be more thoughtful, more energetic, more productive than herself, if they wanted to survive, even in the remaining predominantly black institutions. There were fewer tolerable excuses for not doing so.

12
Invading the World of
Male Scholarship

Marguerite Howie's case illustrates the process by which a black woman entered into an academic profession in the days when it was neither popular nor expected that one did so.[1] No matter what the social environment in which the woman was raised, it did not allow much opportunity for her to aspire to be an academic—a practicing scholar.[2] More likely she would have been expected to move into the more established roles such as teacher, nurse, housewife, or other traditional role set aside for women. If tradition did not have a firm grip on her, trying to juggle the important roles could prove to be quite taxing. Usually, one or the other roles was bound to suffer.

While women today have engaged in movements to gain opportunity to enter practically all the professions, when Howie was ready to become a sociologist, there was no such movement.[3] The woman professor was not firmly established, even in the colleges of the majority group.[4] There were many rules which prohibited the woman from aspiring to a professorial role. It was expected that women would become wives and mothers and this expectation militated against their serious consideration as scholars in higher education. They were discouraged from acquiring terminal degrees on grounds that they would not use them when their services were required within the home. Although a few black colleges had day care facilities, faculty women who were married were not expected to use them. Single women were discouraged from joining the faculties if they had dependent children. Many had to conceal both their marriages and their motherhood until their employment was secure or their status changed.

Only a relatively few women have been able to resolve the tension between rising to their highest professional expectations and managing a home in the time-honored tradition of motherhood and family nurturance. Almost as difficult were the collegiate rules that only one partner could work in a professional capacity at the school.[5] Wives of professors or administrators could be secretaries or members of other ranks not seriously considered or they could work to supplement the incomes of their husbands by holding down the lower, often unranked positions in other departments. Occasionally, they sought employment in fields completely different from education. Some even opened their own businesses.

The latter options were not generally open to black women and they engaged in direct competition with black males for the professorial roles. Oftentimes the women were willing to work for lower salaries than males, which meant a lower valuation of the work they did. Within black society, even if the woman moved into college level teaching, it was not expected that she becomes a scholar. She was to remain a teacher.[6]

Before scholarship was required, women were hired not entirely without consideration for their abilities to add good looks to the campus and faculties. Some of those who were proficient in fields such as the performing arts were allowed some degree of independence for they were protected by specific skills useful to the institution. At Southern black colleges, where most of the women academics were located, women had not begun to conduct research and write books and scholarly papers until well into the 1950s. By that time Howie had been out of undergraduate college for over eleven years. As late as the 1970s young black faculty women were expected to cater parties and activities hosted by the ranking males of their departments. In earlier years, from soon after slavery, black women were expected to perform very important roles in the teaching process. At Tuskegee Booker T. Washington would expect a female teacher to be competent in the household arts for her commission was to train young women for performance in those arts and to teach others once they were out of the school. As black people acquired more rights and were less dependent upon their own resources for their survival and sustenance, their schooling became more general. Less and less did the general subjects require their fullest attention? The teachers of those subjects did not have clear cut missions. In the social sciences the teachers were expected to merely certify that students had been exposed to a state-mandated curriculum which had little to do with the kind of work they would do. At the bachelor's level the task of the social science teacher was not specific. Vague statements might be made that the students were being prepared for further study toward the higher degrees at other institutions outside the South. Since such a small number of students went on to further study, it must be said that the majority of them were not dependent upon their teachers for training them toward social mobility. Without a clear mission, either in teaching, research, or service, the social science teacher could not easily prove that the subject matter proffered was critical.

At the time that the early black women teachers were moving into academic work, neither the black nor the majority communities expected academic work of them. They were there to serve mostly to socialize the students into the more desirable social behaviors. Black colleges expected dormitories and living groups to be overseen by black females. In an illustrative case, a black woman lawyer was placed over a boy's dormitory on a Southern campus. Her opportunity to make a living as a woman lawyer was extremely precarious. The town in which she worked was not large; the black people were escaping the surrounding plantations, taking up living in the least desirable sections of the city, and then under segregated conditions. There were only one or two black male lawyers in the city and they practically monopolized the criminal law practice, there not being much of a civil rights practice. The institution had no need for legal counsel for all decisions which were in doubt were handled by the Board of Trustees which was all white since the college began. When the first black board member was elected in the mid-1950s, the affairs of the college continued to be conducted largely according to custom and precedent.

How, then, did black women scholars find that academic work was expected of them, once they moved into the academic environment? They did not have that many role models, nor were there significant payoffs financially for academic productivity. It remained risky to do too much research or to write books for to do so might suggest that there was lack of agreement of the scholar with the down position of black people. Some administrators thought that their institutions might be economically punished if scholars became productive and competitive with those in the mainstream. Probably only two black schools in the country had created the attitude that scholarship was a social expectation on their campuses. They were Fisk and Howard Universities. Fisk had a tradition developed since its founding in 1867 of promoting liberal thought. Howard, being at the center of the nation's capital, and a federal university, was the seat of a large and relatively well remunerated black bourgeoisie. Howard students always felt advantaged relative to those at other black schools and so did its professors. If a professor gained some experience at Howard, he would be in a better bargaining position to fill an opening at almost any other black school. Howard, arguably, was the top of the line for black education.

But even at Fisk and Howard not all that much academically was expected of either the male or female professors. Their accounting by the federal government was not based on their contributions to scholarship, service, or research, but upon the relationship of the heads of the school to those controlling that aspect of the budget at the federal level. No doubt, because teachers at Howard felt so exalted and were—willy-nilly—the models after which black faculty in other schools of much lesser rank patterned, they were under some pressure to prove their mettle. More-over, there was some competition among themselves at the institution. In schools of the "outback," characterized by scholars such as Caplow and McGee as "Siberian institutions,"[7] scholarship was not a heavy expecta-tion.

The motivation for a female scholar to become productive in an "out-back" institution cannot be accounted for on the basis of either institutional or other normative requirements. It might be argued that her participation in association work, attending meetings and interacting even occasionally with some productive scholars, served to encourage her to make her own forays into the academic groves. Through this process she might gradually incorporate a sense of her own potential productivity. Marguerite Howie served in such institutions for much of her academic career.

Younger women were, of course, socialized much later, especially af-ter the 1960s, in graduate school departments where they were impacted by the civil rights and women's rights movements, both of which placed them on more equal footing with males with whom they competed. As has been stressed at other places in this work, perhaps the two most out-standing black women sociologists of the period of the 1960s were Jacque-lyne Jackson[8] and Joyce A. Ladner,[9] both of whom became productive in the post civil rights movement.

Howie, of course, faced a different set of circumstances than did the later black women scholars. Probably so thorough was the socialization against the productivity of women that she practically gave up the effort until near the end of her career. When Howie became associated with the cooperative research program in the black land-grant system, her studies began to be seen.[10]

13
Howie and Du Bois

When Marguerite completed Shaw University, in 1939, she gravitated toward the teaching field. She passed the examination required for teaching in North Carolina schools, but was too young to receive a teaching certificate. Her option then was to try for further study and wait until she was old enough to receive the North Carolina teacher license. At that time, many of her contemporaries were enrolling in Columbia, especially Teachers College, New York University, and other East Coast graduate schools. Marguerite reports that she wanted to enroll in the University of North Carolina, Chapel Hill. When she submitted her application, she was told that North Carolina would give her a round-trip ticket to any institution she could enter outside the state. Several other Southern states followed this procedure as a means or neither promoting black graduate studies nor permitting the enrollment of blacks in their institutions, where they could receive training not offered in black institutions. Marguerite did not pursue the matter of integrating that institution although there were precedent suits to enter such institutions. Donald Murray had attempted to integrate the Law School of the University of Maryland; Lloyd Gaines had tried to integrate the Law School of the University of Missouri. These efforts occurred in the 1930s.[1] She insists that she did not want to go to any of the previously mentioned states for further study, but was drawn to Atlanta University where she knew W.E.B Du Bois taught.

Du Bois evidently made a great impression on Howie, who stated, as of 1995, that she was probably the last Du Boisian who took classes from him. While there, she was the only woman that Du Bois took under his wing. Believing in the Continental, especially the German method of tutorial instruction, Du Bois would not allow more students in his classes than could get in his office. He was said to be quite eccentric. On occasion, when he invited students to his home for coffee and talk, she noticed that he required his coffee specially ground.

Du Bois was not too fond of having women students in his classes, but Miss Howie (probably Rogers then) easily mustered past Du Bois' standards. She was the only woman student invited to have coffee at the home of the eminent scholar. When she and a male student were in an elevator, either with Du Bois or not, and the matter of grades came up, when Marguerite reported that she received an A from Du Bois, Barnard Robinson, also enrolled in the class, became so chagrined that he slapped Marguerite. The event is said to have provoked a strong reaction from students on the campus who wanted to physically confront Robinson for his indiscretion.[2]

Howie continued to be influenced by Du Bois, even after his death. She reported that she carried two students, two girls, to Ghana, where Du Bois died. They wanted to see his grave and make sure that it was properly cared for. It was not a happy experience for her, evidently. Du Bois' grave had fallen into poor upkeep.[3]

Du Bois' Metaphor of the Talented Tenth

Howie's association with Du Bois casts light upon the character and intentions of that noted scholar in areas not so well understood of him. As a leader of the African American people by then, Du Bois had established a reputation which was public. His confrontation with Booker T. Washington over the direction of black education had become well-known. He was quite noted for his belief that the "talented tenth" would be the leaders of the black people toward establishing them on a par with the rest of the citizenry. It was not simply a numerical proportion of the black population that would have that task. Approximately one-tenth of the black people in the U.S. either had not been slaves or were already freed at the time of the Emancipation Proclamation, or end of the Civil War. By this time, there had been significant miscegenation of the whites and slaves and the freedmen such that about 10 percent or, perhaps, much more, could no longer be identified by their phenotype. These were heavily mixed black people ranging from mulattoes to octoroons and beyond, where very many could pass into the majority category on the basis of phenotype alone. About 10% of the freedmen had some tangible property and were listed on the tax rolls. Another small number, probably at least 10% were formally educated beyond bare literacy by the end of the nineteenth century.

Wherever Du Bois looked, he found a large gap between those freedmen who had some access to the mainstream and those who did not. However the group was divided the results were approximately the same: about 10% were somewhat advantaged and about 90%—the masses of

blacks—were suffering important degrees of disadvantage. It was incumbent upon the advantaged minority of blacks to work to abet and ensure
the advancement of those who were not so advantaged. Since so many
of the advantaged blacks were phenotypically identifiable as of unmixed
African ancestry, it appeared that they were the ones to whom Du Bois
referred as the "talented tenth."[4]

Howie reported that while Du Bois talked a strong game of blackness,
his actions and many thoughts were centered on those who were phenotypically closest to white. He has been criticized for naming the most
prominent black organization the National Association for the Advancement of Colored People at a time when efforts were being made to rees-
tablish some connections to the African heritage. Many organizations, by
1910, such as the African Methodist Episcopal Church, were prefixed with
the word African. This debate continued right up through the Harlem
Renaissance, exampled in the struggle between James Weldon Johnson
and Bishop Alexander Maguire over the issue of whether blacks should be
considered Negroes or Ethiopians. The long nominal independence of the
Ethiopians had thrilled black people for centuries and when the opportunity came, it was almost natural that they would turn toward Ethiopia as
a national role model for much of Africa at this time was yet mired down
in the clutches of colonialism

Yet, Du Bois need not be censured for his thoughts about the important role of the "talented tenth," which some interpreted as a thinly dis-
guised preference for the blacks of lighter skin. Du Bois himself was a
marginalized man who was not comfortable with the social situation in
which he found himself. For the rejection of the black people by the of-
ficials of government, the agricultural and industrial leaders, summarized
as the white people, he had much to fight against. Through his continuing
hope to find something positive in blackness, and then in himself, he had
much for which to fight. He merely represented and reflected the prevailing ideas of that time. As a free thinker it would have been quite difficult
for him to do otherwise.

Marguerite Howie, as a young woman, did not have many models of
women scholars before her, and almost none as formal sociologists. Beyond high school, black education was dominated by men, even if there
was greater gender parity of teachers. Few women, at the national level,
had established themselves with reputations as professors, struggling
with serious academic or technical problems to which they could put
their minds. Women were located largely in those fields in which women
would go upon graduation. Elementary education, home economics, the
secretarial fields, English and, to a lesser extent the social sciences, were
the ones in which the majority of women graduates were found. They

were very few in the natural sciences and even fewer in school administration, either at the secondary or collegiate levels. For much of the time
after the turn of the century, the several levels of black education were
combined under one administration. The early colleges had elementary,
secondary, and collegiate departments. The lower schools generally were
moved from one level to another by the addition of grades until a high
school and even junior colleges were formed.

Sociological study was not encouraged in the South, even at majority
schools. After riots, such as that in Atlanta in 1906, which claimed many
lives, the authorities of Northern cities became restive for they knew the
same tensions existed in their domains. At least, they would make some
effort to study their problems, often utilizing black scholars for this purpose. It was with majority help that Du Bois established the NAACP close
upon the heels of the Atlanta riot. In 1919 riots erupted in Chicago and
other cities. The University of Chicago graduate student Charles S. Johnson was called upon to conduct research into their causes. It is instructive
that schools of the South, such as those in Arkansas, did not see a need to
study the causes of riots, such as the Elaine Riot in Arkansas in 1919 that
took some 26 lives. The governor of the state, a former president of the
University of Arkansas, is said to have collaborated with the Arkansas
National Guard in exceeding their authority in the quelling of the riots.[5]
There is evidence that the Guard itself went on a riot and were uncontrol-
lable in using their power against the sharecroppers.

After the Chicago riot studies, Johnson moved on to New York, where
he edited the magazine *Opportunity*, sponsored by the Urban League. That
organ was intended to provide an outlet for information and programs
aimed at promoting the adjustment of black rural migrants to the city. E.
Franklin Frazier studied riots in Harlem in the 1930s.

When Johnson went to Fisk, in the early 1930s, the depression gripped
the country. The Federal Government was interested in understanding
the black problem in the South for change was in the offing. At the
very time that the depression was deepest, black people were vacating
the plantations, heading for the cities of the South and for the Northern
ghettos. Poverty in the cities combined with discriminated living made a
very volatile mix. Race relations were bound to deteriorate because they
were integrated with poor economic realities. With the ties Johnson had
established at the University of Chicago, and with the Urban League, he
was able to open a center for race relations studies at Fisk. This center
utilized a stream of scholars, from the majority schools, who were willing
to collaborate with Johnson in his studies. Through the center notoriety
followed Johnson. He thus had cover for the conduct of studies, which
was not enjoyed by many other majority or minority scholars in the South.

Similar arrangements were made to a lesser extent with other schools of the South, where studies could be carried out. The late Tilman C. Cothran related how the University of Chicago kept a graduate student at Dillard University who used students to conduct research on changes in the South. Cothran himself was one of those student professors and completed his dissertation using Dillard students as information gatherers.[6]

In all but a few Southern states, sociological scholarship remained proscribed, unless it was conducted as a part of a thesis or dissertation, in which case it was under the direction of a majority-oriented scholar. It was the same in the black institutions. The proscriptions were largely couched in terms of the unavailability of finances for those purposes. Additionally, faculty members were given such heavy teaching and other loads that they had no time or energy for other activities. If a faculty member became too aggressive toward promoting social change, he or she could be fired. The possibility of being blackballed from other schools operating under the same proscriptions discouraged scholarship, not only of the critical variety, but nearly all other as well.

If a woman took up teaching in the secondary schools, there were very few incentives for undertaking scholastic work. Her job was narrowly interpreted so that her principal activity was teaching, or some community service closely related to it. Only during the Harlem Renaissance, when writers such as Zora Neale Hurston and Nella Larsen wrote of the difficulties of living black in the South was there much demand for black women's writing. Women activists, such as Mary McLeod Bethune and Lugenia Burns Hope, though quite prominent socially, were not scholars in the traditional sense of the word, but were more interested in the advancement of black people through moral improvement that would make them more acceptable to the majority group that controlled upward mobility.[7] Some interpreted the political atmosphere as too volatile for such work. Even the studies of eminent male scholars, such as Du Bois and Frazier, were not easily accepted or tolerated by the administrations in the black schools. These administrators believed that their funding might be negatively affected by independent black scholarship that would inevitably be critical of the social environment.

Howie and the Question of Women Scholarship

There was never a very strong academic subculture among women in the African American institutions. Any bonding was based on other criteria usually unrelated to the advancement of academics among the women. It was perhaps almost as weak among the males, a fact that provoked

E. Franklin Frazier to essay against this tendency in his famous *The Black Bourgeoisie*. In these schools, the opportunities may have existed for the exercise of some levels of scholarship beyond preparation for the teaching of classes, but the encouragement to do so was most likely missing. Teaching was something that a qualified instructor was expected to do and there were not many important means of differentiating among teachers beyond disciplines and gender. For much of Howie's higher education teaching career, evaluations of professors by chairs and deans were very informal. Student evaluations of professors were nonexistent or did not carry much weight in administrative circles. There was little use in students' complaining about the performance of a professor without lodging complaints with the chairperson, almost always a male.

If anything, women on the campuses were much more divided than men, for their concerns were traditionally issues over which they could become personally agitated. The concerns of women revolved around issues of home and job, entertainment and, to a lesser extent, religion. If a faculty member, whether male or female, wanted to pursue academic advancement, it was not always taken seriously. Money was very seldom available for the undertaking of research. If it appeared that the scholar might gain some notoriety or recognition, or even cause discussion and the possibility of change within the local community, the research might be discouraged. An institutional research review board that approved proposed research was not necessary in the schools in which Marguerite Howie taught. Administrators performed that function, if informally. Additionally, that faculty member might be penalized by being given additional duties, so that it became less likely that scholastic work would be done.

The development of a subculture of African American women academics came after the women's' revolution in American academics. Majority women were less rankled by what was said against them by majority male scholars, but by their rejection from holding academic posts commensurate with their preparation, especially after publication of such books as Betty Friedan's *The Feminine Mystique*, in the 1960s.[8] Black women, if anything, were more advantaged during the period of official segregation than their black male counterparts. They were the primary breadwinners in their homes because they were not automated out of work in the domestic areas as rapidly as black males were reduced in labor value following agricultural automation and shifts from labor intensive agriculture. Nor were women as much a threat to the economic inequality that was then promoted. There was a lot more status loss in the South when a majority woman had to do her own housework, following the dismissal of her African American maid than when a plantation owner dismissed his tenants. When kitchen appliances became widely available, the Southern white woman resisted using them herself, preferring instead to have black women use them. Standing in the community was important for these women, and that standing depended largely upon their hanging onto the symbols of that status—the employment of a black maid.

Elementary education in the segregated schools was dominated by black women by a ratio of at least 10 to one. Secondary education contained a ratio closer to gender equality while college education contained a ratio advantageous to black males of about 60/40 until well into the 1960s. There were almost no black males in nursing, which traditionally employed a large number of African American females, even when formal training was a lot less rigorous than it is today and certificates not so readily required.

In cities, black males could make more money without formal education than those who achieved formal training up to the bachelor's level. Workers in the industrial plants commonly considered themselves as more prosperous with less education in the North than black teachers in the South who had years of formal education. Status, however, within the black community, always attached to teaching, but this line of work could accommodate only a limited proportion of those who achieved education. Status had to be sought in other areas as well. In the North, where segregation did not exist to the extent it did in the South, black teachers did not have a sinecure and had to compete with other ethnic groups for those jobs. Industrial work was more rapidly automated following World War II, and those without greater skills and formal training for placement in jobs were at risk of unemployment. A greater employment burden fell on black males than on black females leading to the pushing of more of the black males into Professor Wilson's "ghetto underclass."[9]

African American female scholars began to form their own groups, in the 1970s, some later, not so much because they were opposed to the dominance of black males for whom they worked, or perhaps were not allowed to work, but because they did not want to be identified with the majority female issues that stressed the intersection of race, class, and gender. LaFrances Rodgers-Rose's International Black Women's Congress is one such organization that seeks to address academic as well as social issues germane to black women. Black families allied with black males in struggling against the imposition of racial criteria for recognition. Most of them seemed to argue that a struggle against racism would at the same time be one against class and gender making the latter two classes redundant. Black females knew that black males, however well-placed, were not their oppressors in the way that majority males who were powerful were the oppressors of all women.

Howie's trajectory, from early training to productive scholar and social science researcher, to a large extent, is descriptive of that taken by many black women, although there are variations in the finer details for individuals. That she decided to become a productive scholar, with that as her major orientation, is instructive for, in a large sense, she represented a generation of women who took that route. Scholarship is largely silent on how they made their choices. Many of the best known black female writers do so as writers of fiction, a genre that was more favorable to them. This is no doubt why the fiction writers gained greater notoriety than the nonfiction or more empirically based writers. An example of this dichotomy is the career of Margaret Abigail Alexander Walker, who was born in 1915, while Marguerite Howie was born in 1919.[10]

As Howie's record shows, she did not begin to become productive until well into her maturity. That is not unusual. Some black women showed considerable promise as scholars early in their maturity, but gave it up soon thereafter. In addition to having to cope with the raising of children, others, even when they did not have children, were discouraged from productivity in their work settings. There were exceptions to this fact, of course. There does not seem to be any precipitating event in her life, such as a major incident of discrimination that propelled her desire to redress inequities.

James A. Banks reports that much black social scholarship was "vindicationist" in that it adduced data to show that black people were not the inferior people they had been made out to be in some mainstream canonical readings.[11] Howie's inspiration to become a scholar does not seem to have come from any female, or small group of them, either at Shaw University, Atlanta University, or at other institutions where she studied. Although she might have studied at schools that today would be known as research institutions, the greater probability is that they did not expect much by way of research from the black students, whether they were male or female. When some majority scholars discovered that black graduate students had research interests, it was more common for them to become co-opted into the plans of those scholars. Men like Franz Boas thought highly of Zora Neale Hurston at Barnard College, and no doubt encouraged her to do research on black people in the South, in Harlem, and in the West Indies. At Chicago, Robert E. Park co-opted Charles S. Johnson and E. Franklin Frazier. Allison Davis seemed always to be under the sponsorship of John and Mary Dollard. The anthropologist turned thespian Katherine Dunham, was a protégé of noted scholar and black interest anthropologist Melville Herskovits at the University of Chicago.[12] She turned her attention to the Caribbean, most likely on that account. The fact is that these scholars were more likely to be interested in studies of black life if they had dependable sponsorship.

Black women writers may be put into two categories: the writers of fiction and the writers of nonfiction. The fiction writers go back to Phillis Wheatley and continue in an almost unbroken, but evidently interrupted trend until Toni Morrison, Alice Walker and Maya Angelou, to name a few. The nonfiction writers did not make their entry until well into the 1930s. The few women who received master and doctoral degrees, as already noted, were usually writing under the supervision of some majority scholar or minority one with a majority orientation. After attainment of those degrees, the black women settled into niches and generally did not continue their nonfiction writing. Thus, for some years after the 1930s, black women nonfiction writers did not have many role models. Carolyn Bond Day's studies of mulattoes in the early 1930s were impressive enough to be included in Myrdal's work *An American Dilemma*.[13] Day evidently drew the attention of the scholar Ernest Hooton, who tried to revive the thesis of Cesare Lombroso who argued for the idea of "born criminality.[14] Adelaide Cromwell was an early black female scholar whose work on the black upper class in Boston gained some recognition, but it was not published until years later.[15]

Although there is evidence that a number of the early black female scholars at different schools were taken under the wings of established majority scholars and encouraged to conduct work that satisfied the curiosity of these scholars, there is no evidence that Marguerite Howie followed that trail.

Howie and Peer Relations in Sponsorship

When Marguerite Howie was a young woman, there is no question that she fit the pattern of some of the slightly older, but still young black women who were chosen to conduct notable research on the black problem. Their major professors did stand the possibility of finding an interest in them, hopefully as students with some talent, picked them up, and promoted their research. If these young women were in majority schools, such as Zora Neale Hurston's being at Barnard, Katherine Dunham at Chicago, and Carolyn Bond at Harvard, their opportunities may have been better than had they been at black institutions. It is not contended that these women were not genuinely interested in the topics they pursued, but it cannot be overlooked that they were in the position, at least potentially, of being chosen to promote the research of scholars who found interest in them and saw their talent and potential utility. Katherine Dunham may have had a long interest in Jamaican society before going to Chicago, but it was no doubt most certainly enhanced when Herskovits found her talents and enthusiasm interesting. Black professors, such as Du Bois, did not have the resources of the majority ones, and so they could not literally "sponsor" students as it is likely that Franz Boas, Melville Herskovits, and Ernest Hooton did respectively at Barnard, Chicago, and Harvard.

Evidently, by the time that Howie was ready to begin her serious social science studies, there was emerging a shift in attitude of these black women students. The black Civil Rights Movement was encouraging that they look to their own resources and talents and not toward the largesse, goodness, or paternalism of some majority figure. Yet, even on into the 1990s, there is evidence that many black women are not chosen for mobility on the basis of their talents, though these may be substantial, but upon the basis of paternalism of the old variety.

Morehouse College is probably the only mainly black school in the country where the students are literally indoctrinated to carry on in the traditions of those notables who preceded them at the schools.

Summary and Conclusion

Higher education for blacks at the time that Marguerite Howie entered it as a vocation, did not mean what it meant for members of the larger society. The smaller and more isolated the colleges the less they were meaningfully connected to the choices being made affecting higher education. From the very beginning of higher education in America, decisions were made mainly by those who controlled the institutions. When religious groups controlled the colleges, their choices were reflected in the curricula and offerings of the institutions. The creation of a classical Christian conscience was the intent of collegiate level institutions in America from the founding of Harvard in 1636 until around the late 1700s when men like Thomas Jefferson began to challenge the utility of that kind of schooling. It was Dr. Benjamin Rush, the eminent teacher and physician who argued that the old school emphasis needed to be changed to stress the more practical. The hold of the old school foundations so resisted change that Rush advocated a federal university that would be much freer to make curriculum innovations that had more to do with practical living.

After the Civil War when the formal education of black people became problematic, although many schools were begun which stressed a classical curriculum, it was Booker T. Washington's vision of Tuskegee which so captivated the imagination that it became the model of black education for some time after the 1880s. Washington and Du Bois entered into vitriolic debate about the direction which black education should take—Washington stressing the practical and Du Bois the more classical. That debate continued until around 1915 until the death of Washington, but the issue was not settled. The black colleges which were designated land-grant institutions continued to mirror the joint influence of Washington and Du Bois in the curricula they offered.

It was impossible for black educators to solve the problem because they, in general, were not funding the schools. In most cases, even for the private schools, they had little control over the boards. Many of these more than 600 black colleges which were begun, had benevolence as their foundation. States which began black colleges had done so mainly as a means of adhering to the minimum requirements of the law. There was never much intention of having black people receive a competitive education. If they did it was because of their own initiative or due to the untiring efforts of the teachers. These colleges were not looked to as sources of knowledge, though in some cases such that of George Washington Carver at Tuskegee, brilliance and ability to contribute could not be overlooked. Not all of the faculty, even at Tuskegee, were as connected to the outside as was Carver and their contributions were considerably less notable. Teaching at the black college was more like teaching in another world. This statement was just as true at Howard University, the largest and most prestigious of the black institutions, as at the smaller less well-known ones. The focus was not much on answering the hard questions in either areas of natural science or in the arts and social sciences. The real emphasis was upon social life so bitterly described by the sociologist E. F. Frazier in his *Black Bourgeoisie*. If anything, one could literally escape altogether from academic productivity and quality teaching at these institutions, if one had a mind to do so for there were very few means for compelling adherence to the norm of quality teaching or research. The teachers were personalities more than scholars although a small number of teachers at these colleges did what they could to promote scholarship and the life of the mind. To do the latter one had to be driven more by internal than by external controls. There were enormous temptations and incentives to follow the lines of least resistance in teaching and to claim heavy teaching schedules and overwork made it impossible to do research and writing. The flight from public and serious scholarship by faculty members meant that the black college was stamped as a place where teachers were more concerned with the social than with total academic life. Consequently, few scholars at these schools reached the role of truly creative professors although many carried the formal title.

By observation of many in the role, Howie saw the paradox of being designated a professor while not producing as one. She was determined not to fall into that trap. Although the incentives were there to permit and to promote little productivity, she chose to become involved on the mental as well as the physical levels of the professorial role. She wanted to do research and writing and commenting on the problems with which social scientists deal. As soon as was feasible, she got her designation changed to the area of rural sociology, with the department of agriculture at South Carolina State College. As part of a cooperative research program involving several schools, she was able to address some of the problems that were faced by rural peoples as they tried to make the transition to urban living. Her studies were generally state or federally funded. She wanted, however, to meet and address problems that were not within the funding purview of her supporters.

Howie had long been interested in research and scholarly productivity, having had her interest kindled through her association with W. E. B. Du Bois, especially while she was a master's degree student at Atlanta University where Du Bois taught. Tracking Howie's productivity was done in two categories—papers published in journals or as books or monographs, and papers presented at association and other meetings. Those data are as follows:

Table 14.1: Howie's Publication Data[1]		
Year	Published	Papers Presented
1976	1	2
1978	3	3
1979	1	1
1980	0	2
1981	5	4
1982	1	2
1983	2	3
1984	1	2
1985	0	2
1986	2	2
Total	16	23

As enthusiastic as Marguerite Howie was in the prosecution of sociological research, it can easily be observed that the conditions in which she worked were not optimum. Despite those conditions, her contributions are considerably greater than the majority of her contemporaries who practiced in the field as long as she did. Just exerting the effort to remain intellectually active in the schools of the South was difficult. There were simply too many other detractions and discouragements. Added to these difficulties was that of gender. James Conyers notes that about 80% of black American doctorates in sociology received their degrees since 1960. There were only 14 black women sociology doctorates in 1967. That number grew to 103 in 1980.[2] Thus, by the time that black women were ready to compete seriously for the positions in sociology, Howie was a senior scholar who, no doubt, debated the worth of returning to a university for hard study toward a credential that may not have delivered the rewards anticipated.

The prosecution of research has always been difficult in schools of small size and influence, criteria that South Carolina State College met

during Howie's tenure there. The changing mission of these schools, usually meant a decrease in emphasis on the social sciences, especially sociology. Conyers observed that majority institutions continued to employ
black sociologists at a higher rate than black ones. Majority institutions
outbid black ones for the services of black scholars, a trend that been developing since the Civil Rights Movement of the 1950s. By 1967, 42 percent
of black sociologists were employed in majority institutions. That number
increased to 59 percent in 1981.[3]

Marguerite Howie's contribution to sociological research is scattered
in her several writings, as her interests were as varied as the needs of the
people she studied. Her interest was largely upon two aspects of the black
American experience—the rural community and aging. She was keenly
aware of the rural background of the Southern black American, and she
saw clearly that, as rural life was vacated for town and city living, left in
the rurals were senior citizens who did not have the economic or social
vitality to live in the bustling urban area. Many returned to rural areas
where there were few available services. Howie tried to bring attention to
the rural black dwellers and to those who were very aged by being appointed to state boards and commissions that addressed their problems.
Her work is highlighted in a publication entitled *Dimensions of Poverty in
the Rural South*, edited with Jogindar S. Dillon, published in 1968 by the
Center for Community Development and Research, College of Engineering Sciences, Technology and Agriculture, Florida Agricultural and Mechanical University.

Although she was a practicing sociologist, Howie found time to engage in other work. She was undoubtedly one of the main grant–writers
at her institution. Howie's institution, as well as major foundations, found
her writing to their liking. Listed in her vita are a Russell Sage Foundation grant supporting a study of student unrest at historically black colleges, 1966-1968. A Kellogg Foundation grant of $207,000 was awarded
to her institution, largely through her efforts, to develop the Department
of Social Sciences. That grant covered the years 1969-1972. It allowed for
the bringing to the campus of visiting scholars and the offering of semi-
nars in black culture. It subsidized study for faculty members to earn the
terminal degree, while providing in-service workshops for faculty. The
Cooperative Social Science Research Service was a program within the
United States Department of Agriculture to promote the study of rural
life, among its other focuses. Howie wrote several of these grant proposals
and her school received in excess of $600,000 from her efforts.[4]

This study of an early African American woman sociologist has sought
to answer some of the questions raised. It has toured the conditions in
which Marguerite Rogers Howie was raised, her schooling, her ambitions,

and her options, as she was imbedded in her social context. It discusses the major influences in her life and tries to estimate how she dealt with any advantages and ambiguities flowing from attempts to define her within the structure of Southern life. Her adjustment and patterns of resistance are noted. This study is also an inquiry into the role of women in black scholarship at the time of her socialization and suggests that women are yet competing to be taken seriously as academics.

To tell the complete story of the academic life of Marguerite Howie, it has been necessary to discuss the major association to which she gave so much of her time and energy. It is not claimed herein that the life of Marguerite Howie is descriptive of, or characteristic of the lives of other African Americans who sought lives of scholarship and contemplation. Those who have lived as long as she, and who were in similar conditions will, no doubt be able to identify with many of the problems she faced. Like so many women of her time, Howie was expected to hew to narrow options, to limit her aspirations. We have not sought to estimate the psychological cost to her for the choices she made, which were literally forced upon her, but we believe they were great. To our knowledge, Mrs. Howie did not pen her own statement of those personal forces affecting her. Younger women, who contemplate reflective and academic lives, will learn from the experiences of Howie and those of her generation. It is hoped that she will be an inspiration to them. Students in general, will enjoy reading of the work of Marguerite Howie, for it is history and biographical sociology wrapped in a single package.

It is our hope that students will not judge their teachers too harshly until they have walked for a while in their shoes.

Appendix 1

A Few Last Words from Marguerite Howie

During the course of the writing of this work, Marguerite became involved and wrote material that the author feels gives a better feeling of her interest. Her eyesight was failing and she was tiring. Her writing was in longhand. My assistant, Narraca Stubblefield, transcribed the notes to the extent possible. She began to make notes regarding specific pages of one of the manuscript revisions but did not continue. What Marguerite wrote is left as close as possible to its original form. A few author comments are included to improve the flow of her words.

Page xi. Somewhere on this page something should be mentioned about Marguerite Rogers as an undergraduate at Shaw University attended the Association of Social science Teachers in Atlanta. It was there that the sociology component enabled her to interact with undergraduates from Morehouse, Spelman, Hampton, Howard, Tuskegee, Alabama A&M, Jackson State, etc.

The bonds tied here were strengthened when many of the undergraduates were taken by their sponsors to Howard Thurmond's retreat at King's Mountain. For example, each student registered at Shaw University was required to pay one dollar membership in the YM or YWCA. Ergo, as President of the YWCA in 1938, Marguerite Serena Rogers attended the meeting where a cosmopolitan and intellectual exchange among black college men and women prevailed.

The mysticism of a Howard Thurmond impacted on Miss Rogers more than she realized. A quarter century later she found herself at Boston University and attending the services where Dr. Thurmond was Dean of the Chapel.

It was during the 1960s and college students and young faculty members questioned the status quo. The tenor was "Black, Black, Black." It seemed imperative that something drastic had to be done to respond to the demands of students. It was "sizzling hot." in the White Hall auditorium. Each time one of these dignified "yellow" administrators opened his mouth he threw fuel on the fire.

Marguerite says that before she realized what she was doing she moved her way through the crowded aisles to the auditorium platform. "Wait, wait," she shouted. "We are going to Africa. Faculty and students will study in Africa... We will return with art, artifacts, and musical instruments." A dismissal bell rang, the exit music sounded, students and faculty returned to classes gleefully. . . . About six messengers from the President's office rushed up the stairs behind me. "President Nance wants to see you NOW."

Gordon, "If you are going to die, you are going to die... But I had been schooled by the master, W.E. B. Du Bois. I felt like living. I wanted to go to Africa! I wanted to go to Ghana! I wanted to put some flowers on Du Bois's gravesite. I wanted South Carolina State College students to go with me. . . . Instead of being frightened when presidential messengers demanded that I come to his office, I was singing in my heart "I'm going to Africa; were are going to Africa."

"How in God's name am I going to get money to send anyone to Africa?" President Nance yelled as he pranced the floor. I relaxed in one of the plush chairs in his office as if I were chairman of the board.

As quickly as I could I reminded President Nance that the use of money coming from vending machines in the dormitories, at the football stadium, etc., had long been questions each college generation raised..."Now we can answer those questions..."Slush out" the funds for us to go to Africa.!!!

"Mrs. Marguerite," said President Nance, "Let's get down to business. Who, when, where???" As a graduate of Atlanta University, I received the *Journal*, flyers and all such information... An African Study seminar was scheduled for the summer of 1969. American Forum for African Study, a nine graduate credit hour program. There were three alternate options for emphasis and I elected to study the history and culture of Africa. Panel discussions, evening slide lectures, field excursions, dance performances, and other cultural events were held daily. My undergraduate sociology major, Ethel Brown (now Ethel Brown Marshall) completed this course. The professor who taught Black Literature, Mrs. Johnnie Sharpe, and one of her majors, Sandra Bowie, matriculated in the Music, Dance, Arts, Theatre and Literature of Africa.

The band director at S.C.S.C. ordered musical instruments and the University of Ghana packed these and shipped them on our return flight. . . . I sometimes wonder if the instruments are used and cared for us they once were.

The music chairman was Dr. Edwin Christian and his wife is Bennie

Ruth. Christian yet handles the bass at intervals with the Atlanta Symphony but Bennie Ruth has relinquished the books and map making and concentrates on bridge...She will come and pick me up if I'm in Atlanta for ASBS or Rural Sociology.

My citation indicating nine credit hours of study which hangs on my wall is signed by Drs. Lawrence Jones (Program Leader) and C. Eric Lincoln (American Forum for African Study). Mrs. Johnnie Sharpe, Mrs. Ethel Brown Marshall, Mrs. Sandra Bowie, and I each received these. Academic credit was transferred to our institutions of higher learning. ... At S.C.S.C. we were unique in our academic pursuits. Each of us has presented scholarly papers at ASBS stemming from our academic and field research in Africa.

Since I have retired, teachers at Salisbury High School, and church groups, have viewed these slides and use me as a resource person in their classrooms. I am a bit selfish because I will not allow my art and artifacts to go without me (i.e., a gold weight or fertility doll can so easily be lost).

A few years ago, the Charleston Museum borrowed a Harleston and whatever else I would lend. In addition to the Magnolia Garden scene by Harleston, I sent Beauty Untapped by Prof. E. Tetteh of the University of Ghana in Kumasi and a Firedance by Gbegnon of Lome, Togo, West Africa (1969). A firedance is to the village artist as the Madonna was/is to the people who accept Christ (See "The Mystery of Mary" in *Life Magazine*, December 1966).

Great is my love for 1890 institutions. . . . I had just returned from hostessing ASBS (along with Alton Thompson). Ruth Dennis holds forth with undergraduate student papers, but tears stream down my eyes when I face the nightmare that SCSC undergraduates "ain't there no more." There are young people representing Grambling, Morehouse, Howard, Georgia State, Fort Valley, Fisk, Austin Peay, but not S.C.S.C. I am aware that Drs. Simpson and Leonard Goodwin are at S.C.S.C., but they are not alerted to A.S.B.S.

The cause of the inertia, I do not know. I am an emeritus professor and I receive calendars and such, but no human contact. ... When I left, I was giving an undergraduate scholarship. When I retired in 1986, I informed the registrar, Ms. Dorothy Brown, and the chairperson of Honors and Awards, Mrs. Berniece Stukes that I wished to continue the award. They informed me that they had no time for a retiree.

Well, I live in Salisbury. Livingstone College, the only A.M.E.Z. College, is here. Livingstone accepted my scholarship. So for ten years and three different presidents, I have been welcomed at Livingstone. . . . I am recognized at their Samuel E. Duncan Honors Day program and I get a hug from the student who wins the award and his/her parents and/or guardian.

I am an Alpha Kappa Alpha woman, but I do not stipulate Greek affiliation. However, at the 1996 Honors Day at Livingstone I got a hug from an Alpha Kappa Alpha woman.

When I returned from ASBS in Greensboro I received a telephone call from S.C.S.C. that can best be described as "Nope, nope, nope."

I was informed that my presence was desired the following week to receive an honor. I informed Gloria Pyle that I was just returning from A.S.B.S. where Dorothy Cowser Yancey was the W.E.B. Du Bois recipient. I was elated because Ethel Brown, now Marshall, and her husband attended and Patricia Haighler my long life assistant when I was Executive Secretary of A.S.B.S. Pat came with her husband, Ike, and their six month old adopted son (Jeremy Rashad Haighler).

I always believe in bringing family to A.S.B.S. In addition, Dot Yancey's daughter was at the luncheon and my granddaughter and some of her friends from N.C.C.U. in Durham attended. ... And from Salisbury came some Alpha Kappa Alpha women, some neighborhood women, and some Episcopal Church women and one husband. These women are members of the Sarah's Circle, at St. Luke's P. E. Church.

These churchwomen had never attended a professional, predominantly black, national meeting with members from north to south, east to west. The attendance at this meeting is the largest we ever had.

Charles U. Smith, originator of the President's Panel, had experienced some problems getting a full compliment of Black College Presidents. I wrote to "C. U." and suggested certain personages. Of course the magnificent Gloria Scott of Bennett and the chancellor of A and T.

I suggested the learned, articulate interim president of Livingstone College, Dr. Roy D. Hudson, and Dr. Talbert O. Shaw of Shaw University. ... I gave "C.U." a brief resume of my undergraduate participation (1935-1939) and at lunch he told me that "he checked me out" and found such to be valid and decided that it would be wise to come. As additional support I mentioned the late Wilmoth Carter, author of Shaw's Universe (*Shaw University History*) and a resource person I had used as a consultant at our Marriage and Family Life Institute... Wilmoth Carter and Jacquelyne Johnson Jackson were/are two of the most valued and stoic black sociologists.

Page xvii. There was great furor in 1976 when John Griffin, a white candidate was nominated by Charles U. Smith. The powerful persuasive powers of C.U. dominated and the award was given to John Griffin with the futile hope that the said John Griffin would use his influence to funnel some foundation monies in support of A.S.B.S.

"Well, Gordon," said our mentor, "this pipe dream, like all pipe dreams, floated away. . . ." When my husband returned from WW II he found employment at Avery Institute (an American Missionary Association school).

For eons, the AMA institutions were the epitome of classic education among the black middle class. Even today, my neighbor on the street parallel to mine reminds me that she graduated from Avery. I say "Yes, dear, and my husband taught you chemistry." Actually, she is a fine musician and a graduate of W.E.B. Du Bois's Fisk. Ester Commander Marioneaux is her name. She doesn't understand how I can pick up each discordant cadre (cadence) when I don't know one note from another... The answer is that I attended Shaw University; I was required to take nine semester hours of music appreciation under the great Harry Gil-Smythe and my ear "just picks it up." With a classic education one impulsively stands when the first chord is sounded in "The Messiah" and to "Lift every Voice and Sing."

Page 53, re-write. Marguerite Howie was pressured by S.C.S.C. to complete her dissertation at Boston University. The dilemma was that (at) the closest library at the University of South Carolina, the holdings were limited for a dissertation based on the sociology of knowledge and the Boston University Foundations of education thrust. What value would a terminal degree do to foster her research aspirations in Rural Sociology among the black poor in S.C.???

Page 54. She moulded a role.

Appendix 2

Howie, Marguerite Rogers. Vita

PROFESSIONAL DATA: FALL, 1976 -FALL, 1986

EDUCATION

Elementary and Secondary Education, Wilmington, NC.
Shaw University, Raleigh, NC, 1935-1939, A.B., English, French, and History.
Atlanta University, Atlanta, GA, 1939-1941, M.A. - Sociology.
University of Wisconsin, Madison, WI, 1943, 1946—Education and History .
Boston U., Boston, MA, doctoral candidate; prospectus for dissertation approved: 1953, 1959, 1960, 1963 - Social Foundations, Sociology and Guidance.
University of Ghana, Accra and Kumasi, 1969 — Sociology and Culture of Africa.
University of South Carolina, Alcohol and Drug Abuse School, Summer, 1975.
Duke University, Durham, NC, Institute of Gerontology, Summer, 1978.

PUBLICATIONS

"Effects of Communication and Transportation of Utilization of Agency Services by Rural Poor People in South Carolina," *Research Bulletin No. 6*, South Carolina State College, Orangeburg, SC: Cooperative State Research Service, United States Department of Agriculture (January 1976), with Kathleen Hanna.

"What People Say They Do and What they Do: Explorations in the Social of the Rural, Limited Resource Community," *Journal of Social and Behavioral Sciences*, Vol. 2, No. 1 (Winter, 1978), with Kathleen Hanna.

"Communication and Transportation Effects on Agency Use by the Rural Poor," *The Decoder*, Vol. 2, No. 1 (April, 1978).

"How the Rural Poor Choose Agency Services: Communication and Transportation as Factors in the Decision Making Process," Rural Sociology Section Southern Association of Agricultural Scientists: Rural Sociology in the South (Clemson, SC: Clemson University, 1978), with Kathleen Underwood.

Foundations for Self-Determination: A Study of Group Dynamics and Problem Solving Among Rural Poor People: An Experiment in Community Participation, *Research Bulletin No. 13*, South Carolina State College, Orangeburg, South Carolina; Cooperative State Research Service, USDA (May, 1979), with Kathleen Underwood.

"The Role of Knowledgeables in Social Research, Phase 1." Paper presented at the annual meeting of the Southern Association of Agricultural Scientists, Rural Sociology Section, Atlanta, GA, February 4, 1981 (Published in *Rural Sociology in the South*: 1981), with Robert L. Phillips, Jr.

Dimensions of Poverty in the Rural South (Tallahassee, FL: Rose Printing Co., 1986), Library of Congress Catalog Card No. 85-72407, Joint editor with Jogindar S. Dhillon.

Socio-Economic Indicators of Poverty in South Carolina: A Statistical Analysis. *Research Bulletin No. 42*, South Carolina State College, Orangeburg, SC: Cooperative State Research Service, USDA (July, 1986).

PROFESSIONAL PAPERS

"Anomie and Alienation Among Rural, Limited Resource People in South Carolina," New Orleans: Institute of Selected Rural Sociology Researchers in 1862 and 1890 Programs (July, 1976).

"Communications in the Southern Rural Community," Annual Meetings of the Association of Social and Behavioral Scientists, March 23-27, 1978, Hyatt Regency, Washington, D.C.

"Evaluating Community Resources: A Case for Unobtrusive Measures." Paper presented at the Annual Meetings of the Association of Social and Behavioral Scientists, Nashville, TN, March 28, 1980.

"In-Migration and Its Effects on the Quality of Life in South Carolina." Paper presented at the Third Biennial Research Symposium of 1890 Researchers, Atlanta, GA, November 15, 1980.

"An Analytical Study of Research in Behavioral Sciences and Human Nutrition/Rural Development at 1890 Institutions." Paper presented at the annual meeting of the Association of Social and Behavioral Scientists, Atlanta, GA, March 27, 1981.

"Stokely: A Descriptive Analysis of Community Participation." Paper presented at the Southern Sociological Society Meeting, Louisville, KY, April 7-11, 1981.

"A Comparison of Service Delivery Systems Among Community Action Programs in Selected Areas of South Carolina." Paper presented at the annual meeting of the Southern Association of agricultural Scientists, with Robert Phillips, Jr., and Sharon L. Wade. Orlando, Fl, February 2-5, 1986.

"A Profile of Traditional and Nontraditional Agency Users in South Carolina." Paper presented at the annual meeting of the Association of Social and Behavioral Scientists, Inc., Washington, D. C., March 19-21, 1986.

"Reverse or Counterstream Migration in South Carolina." Paper presented at the Annual Meetings of the Rural Sociological Society, Lexington KY, August 17-20, 1983 Published in *Sociological Abstracts*, Vol. 31, No. 5 (December, 1983).

"Values, Attitudes and Beliefs Held by Blacks on Housing Conditions in South Carolina." Paper submitted for presentation at the Annual Meetings of the Association of Black Sociologists, Detroit, MI, August 28-30, 1983.

"Community Development of Coping Skills by Limited Resource Persons in Selected Areas of South Carolina." Paper presented at the annual meeting of the Southern Association of Agricultural Scientists, Nashville, TN, February 5-8, 1984.

"An Assessment of Minority Attitudes on the Quality of Housing in South Carolina: An Exploratory Study." Paper presented at the Annual Meetings of the Association of Social and Behavioral Scientists, Nashville, TN, March 21-24, 1984.

"1890 Regional Research (RR-1) Brochure No. 1: Profile of Rural

Population in 10 Southern States; Utilization of Agency Services," March, 1984.

"A Comparative Analysis of the Duality of agency Delivery with Client Use,." (With Sharon L. Wade and Robert L. Phillips, Jr. Paper presented at the annual meeting of the Rural Sociological Society, College Station Texas, August 22-25, 1984. *Sociological Abstracts*, Vol. 32, No. 3: 57.

"A Temporal Study of Agency Usage in South Carolina: 1973 and 1981. Paper presented at the Fifth Biennial Research Symposium of 1890 Researchers, Dallas, TX, October 23-26, 1984.

"The Use of Physiographic Delimiters in Sampling Techniques for Sociological Research in South Carolina." Paper presented at the annual meeting of the Southern Association of Agricultural Scientists, Biloxi, MS, February 3-6, 1985.

"A Use of Knowledgeables in Rural Research, Phase III." Paper presented at the Annual Meetings of the Association of Social and Behavioral Scientists, Inc., Atlanta, GA: March 27-30, 1985.

CSRS, USDA Grant, "Foundations for Self-Determination," 1976-1978.

"Isolation of Factors: Quality of Life, RR-1" Technical Committee, USDA-1978-present.

"Stokeley: A Descriptive Analysis of Community Participation." Paper presented at the Southern sociological Society Meeting, Louisville, KY, April 7-11, 1981 (With Robert L. Phillips, Jr.). (Published in *Municipal Management: A Journal*, Vol. 4, 1981-1982: 32-35.

"The Role of Knowledgeables in Social Research, Phase 1." Paper presented at the annual meeting of the Southern Association of Agricultural Scientists, Rural Sociology Section, Atlanta, GA, February 4, 1981. (Published in *Rural Sociology in the South*: 1981).

"In-Migration and Its Effects on the Quality of Life in South Carolina." Paper presented at the Third Biennial Research Symposium of 1890 Researchers, Atlanta, GA, November 15, 1980, (With Robert L. Phillips, Jr.). (Published in the Spring 1981 issue of *Explorations in Education at South Carolina State College*. Vol. 18, No. 1: 38-49).

"Evaluating Community Resources: A Case of Unobtrusive Measures."

Paper presented at the Annual Meetings of the Association of Social and Behavioral Scientists, Nashville, TN, March 28, 1980 (with Kathleen H. Underwood and Robert L. Phillips, Jr.). (Published in the *Journal of the Community Development Society*, Vol. 13, No. 2, 1982: 29-41).

"The Use of Knowledgeables in Social Research, Phase II." Paper presented at the Annual Meetings of the *Rural Sociological Society*, University of Guelph, Ontario, Canada, August 19-23, 1981. (With Robert L. Phillips, Jr.) (Published in *Sociological Abstracts*, Vol. 31, No. 5 (December 1983).

"The Role of Volunteerism in Resolving Some of the Problems Associated with Poverty in Rural Communities." Paper presented at the First Sunbelt Economic Opportunity Conference, Greenville, SC, December 11, 1981. (Published in *Proceedings - The First Sunbelt Economic Opportunity Conference: Strategies for Surviving New Federalism in the Sunbelt*, 1982).

"Trends and Characteristics of Return Migrants to Selected Areas of Rural South Carolina," Paper presented at the Annual Meetings of the Association of Social and Behavioral Scientists, Jackson MS, March 25-27, 1982, with Robert L. Phillips, Jr., and Sharon L. Wade (Published in the *Journal of Social and Behavioral Scientists*, Vol. 29).

"Reverse Migration: A Profile of Three Rural Counties in South Carolina," with Robert L. Phillips and Sharon L. Wade. Paper presented at the Fourth Biennial Research Symposium of 1890 Researchers, Orlando, Fl., October 27-30, 1982.

"An Analysis of the Impact of Industrial Development in Selected Counties in South Carolina," with Robert L. Phillips, Jr. and Sharon L. Wade Paper presented at the Annual Meetings of the Southern Association of Agricultural Scientists, Rural Sociology Section, Atlanta, GA, February 6-9, 1983. Published in *Southern Rural Sociology*, Vol. 1.

"Some Psycho-Sociological Aspects of Rural Limited Resource Housing in South Carolina," with Robert L. Phillips, Jr. and Sharon L. Wade. paper presented at the Annual Meetings of the Association of Social and Behavioral Scientists, New Orleans, LA, March 23-26, 1983.

GRANTS

Russell Sage Foundation Grant to do a study of student unrest on historically Negro college campuses, 1966-1968 ($500.00).

Kellogg Foundation Grant to Develop the Department of Social Sciences — 1969-1972 ($207,000).

(a) Visiting Scholar
(b) Seminar in Black Culture
(c) Subsidized study for faculty members to earn the terminal degree.
(d) In-service workshops for all faculty.

CSRS, USDA Grant "Utilization of Communication and Transportation to Effect Agency Utilization Among the Rural Poor," 1973-1976 ($161-048.00).

"Seminar on Black Culture," South Carolina State College, 1968-1975 ($500.00)

CSRS, USDA Grant, Isolation of Factors Related to Levels and Patterns of Living in the Rural South," 1978-1984. ($94,127.00 - October 1, 1980 - September 30, 1981; $108,834.00 - October 1, 1981 - September 30, 1982; $103,884.00 - October 1, 1982 - September 30, 1983; $100,000.00 - October 1, 1983 - September 30, 1984).

CSRS, USDA Grant, "Socio-Economic Indicators of Poverty in South Carolina," 1984-1987. ($80,000.00 - October 1, 1984 - September 30, 1985; $103,500.00 - October 1, 1985 - September 30, 1986).

SOME CONSULTANTSHIPS

South Carolina Commission on Aging, Pre-retirement Council, 1974-1979.

South Carolina Council on Black Aging,   1978-1986.

South Carolina Social Welfare Forum, Executive Board, 1978-1985.

South Carolina Task Force on Aging, 1979-1986.

South Carolina State Coordinating Committee International Women's Year, Outreach Committee Chairperson, 1977.

Human Relations Forum, College of Charleston, March 1980.

President, South Carolina State College Faculty Senate, 1978-1980.

South Carolina State College Faculty Senate, 1969-1973, 1977-1980. Commission on the Future of the South, 1980-1981.

Kellogg Foundation Grant for Department of Social Sciences, 1969-1979, $207,000.

Cooperative State Research Service, U.S. Department of Agriculture Grant, "Foundations   for Self-Determination," 1976-1978.

"Isolation of Factors: Quality of Life, RR-1" Project, USDA, 1978-1986.

Conference on the Black Aging, Washington, D.C. Spring, 1975.

Conference of 1890 Researchers on Regional Projects on "The Development of a Regional   Rural Development Research   Project," Ft. Valley State College, January, 1978.

Joint Legislative Study Committee on Aging, Public hearing Chamber, A Position Statement,   "Agency Utilization and Clients Satisfaction in Reference to South Carolina," October, 1985.

PROFESSIONAL HONORS

Elected to the Directory of American Philosophers.
Who's Who in the South and Southeast, Eleventh Edition.
Who's Who Among American Women, Fifth Edition.
Phi Lambda Theta Honorary Organization for Women in Education.
Alpha Omicron of Alpha Kappa Mu Honor Society
Sigma Rho Sigma Honorary Social Science Society .
Phi Gamma Mu Honorary Social Science Society.
Phi Delta Kappa Honor Society.
Awarded "Distinguished Faculty" Endowed Chair at South Carolina State College, 1982 - 1986.
W. E. B. Du Bois Award, Association of Social and Behavioral Scientists, Inc., 1984.
Morrison-Evans Outstanding Scientist Award, 1985.
Professor Emerita of Sociology, South Carolina State College, May 13, 1986.

PERSONAL MEMBERSHIPS:

American Association of University Professors.
American Sociological Association.
Association for the Study of Afro-American Life and History.
Association of Social and Behavioral Scientists
Rural Sociological Society.
Southern Sociological Society,
South Carolina Sociological Society.
National Association for the Advancement of Colored People, Partici-
pating Life Member
Alpha Kappa Alpha Sorority, Life Member.
National Association of University Women, Orangeburg Branch,
President, 1973-1977.

TRAVEL BEYOND THE CONTINENTAL UNITED STATES:

Canada, 1959;
Puerto Rico and the Virgin Islands of St. Thomas and St. Croix, 1968,
1986.
Ivory Coast, Ghana, Togo and Dahomey, 1969.
Hawaiian Islands, 1970.
West Indies, 1971, 1975

PROFESSIONAL PARTICIPATION:

Visiting Associate Professor, Clemson University, 1971.
Associate Editor, *Journal of Social and Behavioral Sciences*, 1973.
Status of Women in Sociology in the South, Secretary, 1975.
Editorial Board, Explorations in Education, 1963-1986.
Executive Board, Association of Social and Behavioral Scientists, 1976-
present.
Editorial Board, *The Black Aged*, 1975-1979.

DIRECTOR OF REGULARLY SPONSORED PROFESSIONAL
ACTIVITIES:

Marriage and Family Life Institute, 1961-1986.
Presidential Scholar Awards, Chairperson, 1977-1986

ADDITIONAL CIVIC/PROFESSIONAL ACTIVITIES:

Life Membership of NAACP.

Life Membership--Association of Social and Behavioral Scientists.

Liaison person between South Carolina State College and the Greater Orangeburg Chamber of Commerce for the "Community Survey," 1982-1983.

Advisory Committee for International Development Programs at South Carolina State College, 1982-1985.

Appointed by Governor Richard W. Riley as liaison person from State College to enhance and coordinate the Division of Rural Improvement, January 16, 1984-present.

Appointed Chairperson of the Mini-Symposium for Academic Faculty with 1890 Research, December 11, 1984.

Member of Focus Group on Home Economics Curriculum at South Carolina State College, 1985.

Notes

Introduction

1. The conflict between Booker T. Washington and W.E.B. Du Bois over the direction black education should take, in the aftermath of slavery, and in the early decades of freedom is classic. Washington espoused industrial education for the blacks while Du Bois advocated liberal or classical education. For a brief overview of this conflict, see Gunnar Myrdal. *An American Dilemma* (New York; Harpers, 1944), pp. 882-889.

2. See Lorraine Elena Roses and Ruth Elizabeth Randolph. *Harlem Renaissance and Beyond: Literary Biographies of 100 Black Women Writers—1900-1945* (Boston: G.K. Hall & Co., 1990), for an idea of the clustering of the black female writers of the early years.

3. William Leo Hansberry, with Joseph E. Harris. *Africa and Africans as Seen by Classical Writers* (Washington, D.C.: Howard University Press, 1977).

4. George G. M. James. *Stolen Legacy* (New York: Philosophical Library, 1954).

5. Alex Haley. *Roots: The Saga of an African American Family* (Garden City, NY: Doubleday, 1976), is based upon the stories of the griot in the village in the Gambia. In the absence of formal libraries the griot took on the responsibility of remembering the history of the group, its personalities, and critical events. The tradition was carried on in black American communities until well after the Civil Rights Movement when big changes began to affect the community. The role of the old began to change from fountainheads of wisdom, knowledge, and experience, to themselves becoming problems. Now, researchers, writers, and others filled notebooks that filled libraries, leaving the knowledgeable old with reduced roles and influence.

6. See Jacquelyne J. Jackson, "Charles Good Gomillion, Ph.D: A Mighty Social Force," delivered at the annual meetings of the Southern Sociological Society, Atlanta, Georgia, April 8, 1995.

7. O.C. Cox. *Caste, Class and Race* (New York; Doubleday, 1948).

8. The author has tried to tell the late scholar's story in *Tilman C. Cothran: Second Generation Sociologist* (Bristol, IN: Wyndham Hall Press, 1994).

9. Professor of sociology, Indiana State University, Terre Haute, Indiana.

10. Retired professor of sociology at South Carolina State University, Orangeburg, South Carolina.

11 Gordon D. Morgan. *Tilman C. Cothran: Second Generation Sociologist* (Bristol, Indiana: Wyndham Hall Press., 1994).

12. Adelaide M. Cromwell. *The Other Brahmins: Boston's Black Upper Class.* (Fayetteville: University of Arkansas Press, 1994).

13. Carolyn Bond Day. 1932. *A Study of Some Negro-White Families in the United States.* Cambridge: Harvard University Press.

14.. Ida Rowland. *Lisping Leaves* (Philadelphia: Dorrance, 1939).

Chapter 1

1. See Marguerite Rogers Howie, Acceptance Speech: William E.B. Du Bois Award 1984 Annual Meeting of the Association of Social and Behavioral Scientists, Nashville, TN: Sheraton-Nashville Hotel, March, 1984.

2. Charles U. Smith, "Problems and Possibilities of the Predominantly Negro College," Vol. XIII, No. 2, *Journal of Social and Behavioral Sciences*, Fall 1968, pp. 3-8.

3. Blyden Jackson. *A History of Afro-American Literature.* (Baton Rouge: Louisiana State University Press, 1989).

4. For contrasts in the work roles of first and second generation black social scientists, see the author's *Tilman C. Cothran: Second Generation Sociologist* (Bristol, IN: Wyndham Hall Press, 1995).

5. Wesley Clark was a science professor at a black college. He was a veteran and received his terminal degree relatively late. He wanted to teach and not do research at a mainly black institution where the need for teaching was great, and that for research smaller. See "Wesley Clark Dilemma" *Carolina Peacemaker,* circa. 1989.

6. Robert Moran served for long years as a professor of history at Southern University, Baton Rouge, Louisiana.

7. The case study method enables the exploring and analyzing of the life of a social unit, a person, family, institution, cultural group, or community. It seeks to understand the factors accounting for the behavioral patterns of the unit and its relationship to the larger milieu. Charles H. Cooley, a giant of American sociology, was a strong proponent of the use of the case study method. See Pauline V. Young. *Scientific Social Survey and Research* (Englewood Cliffs, NJ: Prentice-Hall, Inc., 1956), p. 299.

8. Although Martineau published in 1837, she did not begin to receive recognition in American sociology until well after the opening of the Civil Rights Movement in the 1950s. See In Richard T. Schaefer and Robert P. Lamm. *Sociology,* Fourth Edition (New York: McGraw-Hill, 1992), and Harriet Martineau. *Society in America. Edited, abridged, with an introductory essay by Seymour Martin Lipset. Garden City, NY: Doubleday, 1962 (originally published in 1837).*

Chapter 2

1. For an excellent account of English settlement in the West Indies at about the same time the Carolinas were settled, see Richard S. Dunn, *Sugar and Slaves:*

The Rise of the Planter Class in the English West Indies, 1624-1713 (New York: W. W. Norton & Co., 1972).

2. See Thomas J. Archdeacon, *Becoming an American: An Ethnic History* (New York: Free Press, 1983), at many places for a history of the Carolinas.

3. This factor had long been noted by authorities. The number of highly mixed African peoples in the mountain states cannot be officially counted. See especially the author's *Black Hillbillies of the Arkansas Ozarks* (Fayetteville: University of Arkansas Department of Sociology, 1972), a report sponsored by the Russell Sage Foundation.

4. Willard B. Gatewood, Jr., *Aristocrats of Color: The Black Elite, 1880-1920* (Bloomington: University of Indiana Press, 1990), is a comprehensive work on the fair-skinned black Americans in various cities and social circumstances.

5. E. Franklin Frazier, *The Black Bourgeoisie* (New York: Collier Books, 1957).

6. Gatewood, op. cit., p. 339 and especially Chapter 12.

7. The story of the origin of color and the problems and prospects its focus entailed has been told many times. See Adele Logan Alexander. 1991. *Ambiguous Lives: Free Woman of Color in Rural Georgia, 1789—1879* (Fayetteville: University of Arkansas Press, 1991), for a story of how one family of women met this challenge, including the outcomes of their offspring.

8. The author's *Ida Rowland Bellegarde: Master Teacher/Scholar* (New York: McGraw-Hill, 1992), gives some attention to how these persons tried to manage their lives, often living as obscurely as possible before it became fashionable to become involved in direct civil rights work.

9. See Keneth Kinnamon, "Native Son: The Personal, Social, and Political Background." *Phylon: Review of Race and Culture,* Spring , 1969, pp. 66 - 72.

10. There has emerged a new interest in the problems of color among minority groups. It was thought that this issue diminished in significance during the Civil Rights Movement when black people were unified behind the banner "black is beautiful." See Naomi Zack, Ed., *American Mixed Race: The Culture of Microdiversity* . Lanham, MD: Rowman & Littlefield, 1995).

11. Everett V. Stonequist, *The Marginal Man* (New York: Scribner's Sons, 1937).

12. See Gunnar Myrdal, *An American Dilemma* (New York: Harper and Brothers Publishers, 1944), especially the notes to Chapter 31 on caste and class, pp. 1374-1380.

Chapter 3

1. "The ASBS: A Historical Sketch," in the Program, Annual Meetings, March 24-27, 1993, Cleveland, Ohio, p. 7.

2. Ibid., p. 7.

3. Ibid., p. 7.

4. See Walter Rodney. *How Europe Underdeveloped Africa.* (Washington, D.C.: Howard University Press, 1974).

5. There were several black towns, such as Nicodemus, Kansas, Kinloch, Missouri, Robbins, Illinois, Menifee, Arkansas, Boley, Oklahoma, and Mound Bayou, Mississippi. Towns like Wilberforce, Ohio were substantially black.

6. See the "Demise of the Black Educator," *ASBS Journal.*

7. In some Southern states black teachers were required, under pain of job loss, to belong to both the Negro and white teacher associations, though they could participate only in their own.

8. The author was a member of a two-person department of sociology from 1965-1969 in a state supported land-grant institution established for blacks shortly after the Civil War.

10. Other journals were founded but publication in them was much more local than those mentioned.

Chapter 4

1. The following are just some of the works of Charles H. Wesley: *The Negro in Our History.* (With Carter G. Woodson). (Washington, D.C. Associated Publishers, 1962); *The Negro in the Americas* (Washington, D.C.: Graduate School, Howard University, 1940); *The Collapse of the Confederacy* (Washington, D.C.: Associated Publishers, 1937); *Freedom's Footsteps: From the African Background to the Civil War* (New York: Publishers Co.,1968); *Neglected History: Essays in Negro History by a College President* (Wilberforce, OH: Central State College Press, 1965).

2. See G. Franklin Edwards. "The Contributions of E. Franklin Frazier to Sociology," *Journal of Social and Behavioral Sciences*, Vol. XIII, No. 1, Winter 1967, pp. 25-29.

3. Frazier's bibliography is found in G. Franklin Edwards (*E. Franklin Frazier on Race Relations*. Chicago: The University of Chicago Press,1968), pp. 325-331.

4. Richard Robbins, "Shadow of Macon County: The Life and Work of Charles S. Johnson," *Journal of Social and Behavioral Sciences*, Vol. XVIII, Nos. 1 & 2, Fall & Winter, 1971-1972, pp. 21-26.

5. For information covering the life and work of Charles G. Gomillion, see Jacquelyne Johnson Jackson, "Charles Good Gomillion, Ph.D.:A Mighty Social Force," delivered at the annual meetings of the Southern Sociological Society, Atlanta, Georgia, April 8, 1995.

6. Ralph Hines, "The Negro Scholar's Contribution to Pure and Applied Sociology," *Journal of Social and Behavioral Sciences*, Vol. XIII, No. 1, Winter 1967, pp. 30-35.

7. John Kammin, "The Discipline of Sociology: Changes Over the Past Twenty Years," an Independent Study Report, Department of Sociology, University of Arkansas, Fayetteville, Arkansas, 1994.

Chapter 5

1. See Lorraine Elena Roses and Ruth Elizabeth Randolph, *Harlem Renaissance and Beyond: Literary Biographies of 100 Black Women Writes: 1900-1945* (Boston, MA: G.K. Hall, 1990), pp. 77-79.

2. Ellen Irene Diggs. *Black Chronology: From 4000 B.C. to the Abolition of the Slave Trade* (Boston: G.K. Hall, 1983).

3. See Gordon D. Morgan. *Ida Rowland Bellegarde: Master Teacher/Scholar* (New York: McGraw-Hill, 1990).

4. The work of Charlotte Hawkins Brown is discussed in Jacquelyne Johnson Jackson, "Black Women in Higher Education," Seminar in Black Culture, 1968-1974, Orangeburg, South   Carolina: South Carolina State College, pp. 1-36).

5. Discussed in Jacquelyne Rouse. *Lugenia Burns Hope* (Athens, GA: The University of Georgia Press, 1990).

6. Information to be released from the *North Carolina State of Colored People*, 1200 Arlington   Street, Greensboro, NC 27401 (919) 274-0851.

7. Ibid. See also Geltner Simmons, "NAACP Suing Schools," *The Salisbury Post*," Friday, June 7, 1991, pp. 1 & 2.

Chapter 6

1. C.U. Smith, Ed., *Social Unrest at Historically Black Colleges* (Silver Spring, MD: Beckham House Publishers, Inc., 1994), p. 81.

2. See Gordon D. Morgan, "African Survivals in the Black Subculture: The Debate Reopened," *Journal of the Association of Social and Behavioral Scientists*, 1977.

3. Carter, et al., in C.U. Smith, Ibid., p. 83.

4. Harry Edwards, *Black Students* (New York: Free Press, 1970), p. 1.

5. The Executive Order 8802 and its relationship to the origin of the Fair Employment Practice Committee, initiated by President Franklin D. Roosevelt is reviewed in Gunnar Myrdal, *An American Dilemma* (New York: Harper and Brothers, 1944), pp. 414—415.

6. The travails and psychological turmoil of the middle class black flowing from the quest for security in the majority culture is discussed in Edwards, Chapter 1.

7. Gunnar Myrdal, op. cit., notes that it was a chance for black youth to learn of the rebellion of some of their forbears who resisted slavery. Some say they were thought more dangerous with this kind of information.

8. Much of the protest of black slaves is found in novel writings that mirror the experiences of the time, in works such as Harriet Beecher Stowe's *Uncle Tom's Cabin.*

9. Aldon D. Morris, *The Origins of the Civil Rights Movement: Black Communities Organizing for Change* (New York: Free Press, 1984), pp. x—xi, notes that out of their persistent struggles a protest tradition arose among blacks that includes hundreds of slave revolts, the underground railroad, numerous protest organizations, the Garvey Movement, and A. Philip Randolph's March on Washington Movement. The 1995 March on Washington, led by Minister Louis Farrakhan continues that tradition.

10. George E. Simpson and J. Milton Yinger, *Racial and Cultural Minorities: An Analysis of Prejudice and Discrimination*, 4th Ed. (New York: Harper & Row, Publishers, 1972), p. 594.

11. Ibid.

12. See Gordon D. Morgan and Izola Preston, *The Edge of Campus: An Informal Social History of Blacks at the University of Arkansas* (Fayetteville: University of Arkansas Press, 1990).

13. Quoted in Aldon D. Morris, p. 27, who refers to Benjamin Muse, *Ten Years of Prelude* (New York: Viking Press, ¡964), pp. 8—15.

14. Samuel B. Gould, President of the State University of New York, "The Uni-

versity and State Government: Fears and Realities," in John Minter, Ed., *Campus and Capitol* (Boulder: Western Interstate Commission for Higher Education, 1966), pp. 3—15, offers a very cogent understanding of the power of the state governor in setting education policy and direction in a state. See also Spurgeon M. Stamps and James C. Renick, "Leadership Styles of the Black College President: An Area in Need of Elaboration," Interdisciplinary Social Sciences, University of South Florida. No date given.

15. See Aldon Morris, p. 201.

16. Leroy D. Clark, "Leadership Crisis: A New Look at the Black Bourgeoisie," *Freedomways*, 3rd. Quarter (Summer 1968): 215—225.

17. From "Black Colleges: Plight or Promise," Pine Bluff Commercial, December 6, 1972, p. 4.

Chapter 7

1. DeLois Gibson, *A Historical Study of Philander Smith College, 1877-1969 (Fayetteville: University of Arkansas, 1972), Ed. D. thesis.*

2. Elizabeth Jacoway. *Yankee Missionaries in the South: The Penn School Experiment* (Baton Rouge; Louisiana State University Press, 1980). See also Fletcher Green. *The Role of the Yankee in the Old South* (Athens: University of Georgia press, 1972).

3. John Munroe was a distinguished dean of freshmen students at Yale University in the late 1960s or early 1970s when he decided to change his location.

4. It has been observed in other connections that whites go through certain stages in work with blacks. These stages are contentment, indignation, awkwardness, and dismay in interracial work. See C.J. levy. *Voluntary Servitude (New York; Appleton-Century Crofts, 1968).*

Chapter 8

1. We use the concept Atlanta Complex to denote institutions of the area: Morehouse, Spelman, Morris Brown, Atlanta University, and the Interdenominational Seminary, all traditional black schools.

2. A good work that emphasizes the role of women in the teaching of students at the black college level is seen in Jacqueline Anne Rouse. *Lugenia Burns Hope: Black Southern Reformer (*Athens: University of Georgia Press, 1989).

3. The Little Rock Nine is the title given to the nine students who integrated Little Rock (Arkansas) Central High School in 1957 forcing President Dwight D. Eisenhower to override the orders of Governor Orval E. Faubus and post Federal troops for a year to ensure their enrollment.

4. Patricia Hill Collins and Margaret Anderson. *Race, Class, and Gender: An Anthology* (Belmont, CA: Wadsworth Publishing Co., 1992), p. 387.

5. Mr. Reed, now late, was a political scientist who taught for many years at the University of Arkansas, Fayetteville, as well as at other schools. He was well noted for his observations and commentary on social and economic conditions of various groups in America. The above notes are from discussions with Professor Reed over the years.

6. Individuals are influenced by the general ideas abroad in their own age. See John C. Green. *The Death of Adam: Evolution and Its Impact on Western Thought.* (Ames, Iowa: The Iowa State University Press, 1959). Preface.

7. Ibid.

8. John Ray. Synopsis, Methodica Stirpium Britinnacarum; tum Indigenis, tum in Argris Cultis locis suis dispositisis; Additis generum Characteristics, specierum descriptionibus & virium epitome (London; Impesis G & J Innys, 1724).

9. Albert Memmi. *The Colonizer and the Colonized* (Boston: Beacon Press, 1965), p. xii, believes that the fundamental difference between the colonizer and the colonized is the colonizer's assumption of privilege, or superiority relative to the colonized.

Chapter 9

1. This is a euphemism for maintenance of the presumed position of black subordination in any dealings with members of the white majority.

Chapter 10

1. Frederick Rudolph. *The American College and University: A History* (New York: Random House, 1962), p. 176.

2. See Page Smith. *Killing the Spirit: Higher Education in America* (New York: Penguin, 1962).

3. We found very little on the culture of the university or of college administrators in Everett C. Ladd, Jr., and Seymour M. Lipset. *The Divided Academy: Professors and Politics* (New York: W.W. Norton & Co., 1975), a comprehensive work on the academic environment. See also Burton J. Bledstein. *The Culture of Professionalism: The Middle Class and the Development of Higher Education in America* (New York: W.W. Norton & Co., 1976), which exhibits the same silence on issues and problems of the culture of higher education administrators.

4. The history of I.Q testing is found in Richard J. Herrnstein and Charles Murray. *The Bell Curve: Intelligence and Class Structure in American Life* (New York: Simon & Schuster, 1994).

5. The story of O.C. Cox's conflict with American sociology has not been told. Snippets of it are found in Herbert M. Hunter and Sameer Y. Abraham, eds. *Race, Class, and the World System: The Sociology of Oliver C. Cox* (New York: Monthly Review Press, 1987). Although Cox is a most distinguished graduate of the department of sociology of the University of Chicago, the press of that institution has not shown any interest in bringing out a major work on him. See the author's "First Generation Black Sociologists and Theories of Social Change," *Journal of the Association of Social and Behavioral Scientists,* 1974.

6. If Marguerite Howie is treated as a second generation social scientist, the tradition had not then arisen for these scholars to write down or to publish their experiences, even in the cheapest form on their campuses. The stories they told were changed and embellished from one telling to the next. The present author, working in a predominantly black school under the stress of change, in the mid-1960s, had to tell his story of upward mobility from poverty in Central Arkansas to

a professorship so often he published, in a very economical form, *Poverty Without Bitterness; Growing up in Central Arkansas* (Jefferson City, Missouri: New Scholars Press, 1970).

Chapter 11

1. The idea of the exploitation of women seemed to be the foundation of the Women's Liberation Movement. See Angela Y. Davis. *Women, Race, and Class* (New York: Random House, 1983), pp. 222-224..

2. Ibid., p. 225

3. The nature of the sociological generation is found in Gordon D. Morgan. *Tilman C. Cothran: Second Generation Sociologist* (Bristol, IN: Wyndam Hall Press, 1994).

4. See Helen M. Lynd. *England in the Eighteen-Eighties: Toward a Social Basis for Freedom* (New York: Oxford University Press, 1945), as an example of the work of an early female sociologist.

5. Mary R. Gardner worked with Allison Davis and her husband Burleigh Gardner on studies of Southern culture. She probably never attained independence from male supervision. See Allison Davis and Burleigh Gardner and Mary Gardner. *Deep South* (Chicago: University of Chicago Press, 1941).

6. Gordon D. Morgan. *Ida Rowland Bellegarde: Master Teacher/Scholar* (New York: McGraw-Hill, 1992), studies the life of one of the early female scholars of social science.

Chapter 12

1. Ellen Irene Diggs, born in 1906, wanted to make a reputation as a scholar, but found it difficult to do so. Her work at Morgan State College was perhaps never fully regarded. See her *Black Chronology: From 4000 B.C. to the Abolition of the Slave Trade* (Boston: G.K. Hall, 1983), for an example of the quality of her work.

2. Black women nevertheless were quite intellectually productive but much of their scholastic and artistic work did not make it into print. Lorraine Elena Roses and Ruth Elizabeth Randolph. *Literary Biographies of 100 Black Woman Writers 1900-1945* (Boston: G. K. Hall & Co., 1990) have sought to bring to light some of the work of the black female writers.

3. Studies have begun to emerge on the backgrounds of black sociologists. In these studies black females have not been highly represented. See James E. Conyers, "Negro Doctorates in Sociology." *Phylon*, 22:209-23, and his "Who's Who Among Black Doctorates in Sociology," *Sociological Focus*, vol. 19, no. 1 (January 1986): 77-93.

4. It is only recently that even the major sociological establishment has begun to honor female scholars. Practically no women were functioning as prominent sociology scholars prior to 1950. See Howard W. Odum. *American Sociology: The Story of Sociology in the United States Through 1950* (New York: Longmans, Green and Co., 1951), where evidence offered will substantiate this point.

5. These rules were in place in many schools. And while they may not have been formally written down, they were operative and can be verified by persons

who worked in the schools of the time. One example of such school was Langston University of Oklahoma.

6. The story of one black woman's attempt to become a part of a male dominated department of social sciences is seen in the author's *Ida Rowland Bellegarde: Master Teacher/Scholar* (New York: McGraw-Hill, 1992).

7. Theodore Caplow and Reece McGee, *The Academic Marketplace* (New York: Basic Books, 1958).

8. Jacquelyne Jackson received her Ph.D. at The Ohio State University in 1960 and began her productivity soon thereafter, working at black institutions such as Tennessee State University (Nashville, Tennessee) and Southern University (Baton Rouge, Louisiana). Later, she worked at Howard University (Washington, D.C.) but was unfulfilled there. She moved to Duke University Medical School and found some difficulty in being promoted. Although admittedly an excellent and productive scholar, Jackson deviated substantially from expectations for a black woman scholar and her mobility was somewhat compromised. In addition to her many articles, her *Minorities and Aging* (Belmont, CA: Wadsworth, 1980), was highly regarded as a critical statement on the many aspects of black aging.

9. Joyce A. Ladner was one of the bright young women scholars of the post–Civil Rights Movement. She received her Ph.D. at Washington University, St. Louis, and worked with some of the more aggressive young scholars at that institution. Probably the atmosphere at Washington University was open enough for Ladner to feel comfortable instead of threatened. Her book, *Tomorrow's Tomorrow* (Garden City, New York: Doubleday, 1971), became a highly respected work on the subject of black women and the Afro–American family. She edited *The Death of White Sociology* (New York: Random House, 1973).

10. Joghinder Dillon and Marguerite R. Howie, Editors. *Dimensions of Poverty in the Rural South* (Tallahassee, Florida: Center for Community Development and Research. College of Engineering, Sciences, Technology & Agriculture, 1986).

Chapter 13

1. Clyde Clarence Ferguson and Albert P. Blaustein. *Desegregation and the Law: The Meaning and Effect of the School Desegregation Cases* (New York: Vintage Books, 1962), probably contains the classic statement and analysis of these cases. See also Mary Caroline Procter, "A History and Analysis of Federal Court Decisions in School Desegregation Cases; Implications for Arkansas." Ph.D. thesis. University of Mississippi, 1992, for a description of these cases and their conclusions.

2. Personal discussion with Marguerite Howie by telephone, September, 1995.

3. Howie described her relationship with and feelings about Du Bois in the telephone conversation, supra.

4. Du Bois' "talented tenth" notion has been much discussed, especially in his confrontation with Booker T. Washington. See Henry Lee Moon. *The Emerging Thought of W.E.B. Du Bois* (New York: Simon and Schuster, 1972), at several places, where the concept is discussed.

5. See D.B. Gaines. *Racial Possibilities as Indicted by the Negroes of Arkansas* (Little Rock, AR; Philander Smith College Printing Department, 1896).

6. See Tilman C. Cothran "Negro Conceptions of White People." Ph.D. dissertation. University of Chicago, Department of Sociology, 1949.

7. See Jacqueline Anne Rouse. *Lugenia Burns Hope: Black Southern Reformer* (Athens: University of Georgia Press, 1989), which discusses the work of these early black community and school leaders.

8. Betty Friedan. *The Feminine Mystique* (New York: Norton, 1963), is said to have sparked the debate and national action commonly known as the Women's Liberation Movement.

9. See William Julius Wilson. *The Truly Disadvantaged* (Chicago: University of Chicago Press, 1988), for an elaboration of this concept.

10. See Lorraine Elena Roses and Ruth E. Randolph. *Harlem Renaissance and Beyond: Literary Biographies of 100 Black Women Writers, 1900-1945* (Boston: G.K. Hall & Co., 1990), pp. 332-336

11. See James A. Banks, "The Historical Reconstruction of Knowledge About Race: Implications for Transformative Teaching," *Educational Researcher*, March 1995, pp. 15-25.

12. Roses and Randolph, op. cit., pp. 94-97.

13. Carolyn Bond Day. *A Study of Some Negro-White Families in the United States* (Cambridge, Mass.: Peabody Museum of Harvard University, 1932).

14. See George B. Vold. *Theoretical Criminology*, 2nd Edition (New York: Oxford University Press, 1979), pp. 36-40. Hooton was greatly influenced by the thought of Lombroso and probably sought support for this thinking in the studies of Carolyn Bond Day, then a youthful, bright and even impressionable young woman at Harvard.

15. Adelaide M. Cromwell. *The Other Brahmins: Boston's Black Upper Class, 1750-1950* (Fayetteville: University of Arkansas Press, 1994).

Summary and Conclusion

1. Taken from Howie's Vita, which she generously provided the author.

2. James E. Conyers, "The Employment of Black Doctorates in Sociology," a paper presented at the Annual Meetings of the American Sociological Association, Washington, D.C., August, 1985.

3. Ibid.

4. Data taken from Vita of Marguerite Rogers Howie.

Bibliography

Alexander, Adele Logan. *Ambiguous Lives: Free Women of Color in Rural Georgia, 1789-1879* (Fayetteville: University of Arkansas Press, 1991).

Banks, James A., "The Historical Reconstruction of Knowledge About Race: Implications for Transformative Teaching," *Educational Researcher*, March 1995.

Bledstein, Burton J. *The Culture of Professionalism: The Middle Class and the Development of Higher Education in America* (New York: W.W. Norton & Co., 1976).

Brameld, Theodore. *The Remaking of a Culture* (New York: Harper and Brothers, Publishers, 1959).

Caplow, Theodore and Reece McGee. *The Academic Marketplace* (New York: Basic Books, 1958).

Clark, Leroy D., "Leadership Crisis: A New Look at the Black Bourgeoisie," *Freedomways*, 3rd Quarter (Summer 1968).

Collins, Patricia Hill and Margaret Anderson. *Race, Class, and Gender; Anthology* (Belmont, CA: Wadsworth Publishing Co., 1992).

Conyers, James E., "Who's Who Among Black Doctorates in Sociology," *Sociological Focus*, Vol. 19, No. 1 *(January 1986)*.

Conyers, James E., "Negro Doctorates in Sociology," *Phylon*, 22:209-23.

Cothran, Tilman C. "Negro Conceptions of White People." Ph.D. dissertation. University of Chicago, Department of Sociology, 1949).

Cromwell, Adelaide M. *The Other Brahmins; Boston's Black Upper Class, 1750-1950* (Fayetteville: University of Arkansas Press, 1994).

Davis, Angela Y. *Women, Race, and Class* (New York: Random House, 1983).

Davis, Allison and Burleigh Gardner and Mary Gardner. *Deep South* (Chicago: University of Chicago Press, 1941).

Day, Carolyn Bond. *A Study of Some Negro White Families in the United States* (Cambridge, MA: Peabody Museum of Harvard University, 1932).

Diggs, Ellen Irene. *Black Chronology: From 4000 B.C. to the Abolition of the Slave Trade* (Boston: G.K. Hall, 1983).

Dillon, Jogindar and Marguerite R. Howie, Eds. *Dimensions of Poverty in the Rural South* (Tallahassee, Florida: Center for Community Development and Research, College of Engineering, Sciences, Technology and Agriculture, 1986).

Dunn, Richard S. *Sugar and Slaves: The Rise of the Planter Class in the English West Indies, 1624-1713* (New York: W.W. Norton & Co., 1972).

Edwards, Harry. *Black Students* (New York: Free Press, 1970).

Edwards. G. Franklin, "The Contributions of E. Franklin Frazier to Sociology," *Journal of Social and Behavioral Sciences,* Vol. XIII, No. 1, Winter 1967.

Ferguson, Clyde C., and Albert P. Blaustein. *Desegregation and the Law: The Meaning and Effect of he School Desegregation Cases* (New York: Vantage Books, 1962).

Frazier, E. Franklin. *The Black Bourgeoisie* (New York: Collier Books, 1957).

Freedom's Footsteps, From the African Background to the Civil War (New York: Publishers Co., 1968).

Friedan, Betty. *The Feminine Mystique* (New York: Norton, 1963).

Gaines, D.B. *Racial Possibilities as Indicated by the Negroes of Arkansas* (Little Rock, AR: Philander Smith College Printing Department, 1896).

Gatewood, Willard B., Jr. *Aristocrats of Color: The Black Elite, 1880-1920* (Bloomington: University of Indiana Press. 1990).

Goldsby, Richard A. *Race and Races,* 2nd Ed. (New York; Macmillan Publishing Co., Inc., 1977).

Greeley, Andrew. *Ethnicity in the United States: A Preliminary Reconnaissance* (New York: Wiley, 1974).

Green, John C. *The Death of Adam: Evolution and its Impact on Western Thought* (Ames, Iowa: The Iowa State University Press, 1959).

Harris, Trudier, Ed. *Afro-American Writers from the Harlem Renaissance to 1940* (Detroit, Michigan: Gale Research Co., 1987).

Herrnstein, Richard J., and Charles Murray. *The Bell Curve: Intelligence and Class Structure in American Life* (New York; Free Press, 1994).

Hines, Ralph, "The Negro Scholar's Contribution to Pure and Applied Sociology," *Journal of the Social and Behavioral Sciences,* Vol. XIII, No. 1, Winter 1967.

Hunter, Herbert M., and Sameer Y. Abraham, Eds. *Race, Class, and the World System: The Sociology of Oliver C. Cox* (New York: Monthly Review Press, 1987).

Jensen, A.R., "How Much Can We Boost I.Q. and Scholastic Achievement?" *Harvard Educational Review, 1969.*

Johnson Jackson, Jacquelyne , "Charles Good Gomillion, Ph.D.: A Mighty Social Force," delivered at Southern Sociological Society, Atlanta Georgia, April 8, 1995.

Kammin, John, "The Discipline of Sociology: Changes over the Past Twenty Years,' an Independent Study Report, Department of Sociology, University of Arkansas, Fayetteville, Arkansas, 1994.

Kinnamon, Keneth, "Native Son; The Personal, Social and Political Background," *Phylon: Review of Race and Culture,* Spring 1969.

Ladd, Everett C., Jr., and Seymour M. Lipset. *The Divided Academy: Professors and Politics* (New York: W.W. Norton & Co., 1975).

Ladner, Joyce A., Ed. *The Death of White Sociology* (New York: Random House, 1973).

Levin, Roger. *Bones of Contention: Controversies in the Search for Human Origins* (New York: Simon and Schuster, 1987).

Lynd, Helen M. *England in the Eighteen-Eighties: Toward a Social Basis for Freedom* (New York: Oxford University Press, 1945).

Memmi, Albert. *The Colonizer and the Colonized* (Boston: Beacon Press, 1965).

Minter, John, Ed. *Campus and Capitol* (Boulder, Colorado: Western Interstate Commission for Higher Education, 1966).

Moon, Henry Lee. *The Emerging Thought of W.E.B Du Bois* (New York; Simon and Schuster, 1972).

Morgan, Gordon D., and Izola Preston. *The Edge of Campus: An Informal Social History of Blacks at the University of Arkansas* (Fayetteville: University of Arkansas Press,1990).

Morgan, Gordon D. *Poverty Without Bitterness: Growing up in Centrtal Arkansas* (Jefferson City, Missouri: New Scholars Press, 1970).

Morgan, Gordon D. *Tilman C. Cothran: Second Generation Sociologist*(Bristol, IN: Wyndham Hall Press, 1994).

Morgan, Gordon D. *Ida Rowland Bellegarde; Master Teacher/Scholar* (New York: McGraw-Hill, 1992).

Morgan, Gordon D. *Marianna* (Fayetteville, AR: New Scholars Press, 1972).

Moynihan, Daniel Patrick. *The Negro Family: The Case for National Action* (Washington, D.C.: Department of Labor, Office of Planning and Research, 1965).

Myrdal, Gunnar. *An American Dilemma* (New York: Harper & Brothers, 1944).

Odum, Howard W. *American Sociology: The Story of Sociology in the United States Through 1950* (New York: Longman, Green and Co., 1951).

Procter, Mary Caroline, "A History and Analysis of Federal Court Decisions in School Desegregation Cases: Implications for Arkansas." Ph.D. thesis. University of Mississippi, 1992.

Ray, John. *Synopsis methodica stirpium britnnicrum; tum Indigenis, turm in Argis Cultis locis suis dispositisis; additis generum Characteristics, specierum descriptionibus & virium epitome* (London; Impesis G & J Innys, 1724).

Riesman, David and Christopher Jencks, "The American Negro College," *Harvard Educational Review, Winter 1987.*

Robbins, Richard, "Shadow of Macon County: The Life and Work of Charles S. Johnson," *Journal of Social and Behavioral Sciences,* Vol. XVIII, Nos. 1 & 2, Fall & Winter, 1971-1972.

Rodney, Walter. *How Europe Underdeveloped Africa* (Washington, D.C.: Howard University Press, 1974).

Roses, Lorraine Elena and Ruth Elizabeth Randolph. *Harlem Renaissance and Beyond; Literary Biographies of 100 Black Women Writers: 1900-1945* (Boston: G.K. Hall & Co., 1990).

Rouse, Jacqueline Anne. *Lugenia Burns Hope; Black Southern Reformer* (Athens; University of Georgia Press, 1989).

Rudolph, Frederick. *The American College and University: A History* (New York: Random house, 1962).

Simmons, Geltner, "NAACP Suing Schools," *The Salisbury Post,"* Friday, June 7, 1991, pp. 1 & 2.

Simpson, George E., and J. Milton Yinger. *Racial and Cultural Minorities: An Analysis of Prejudice and Discrimination, 4th Ed* (New York: Harper & Row, Publishers, 1972).

Smith, Charles U., "Problems and Possibilities of the Predominantly Negro College," *Journal of the Association of Social and Behavioral Sciences,* Vol. XIII, No. 3, Fall 1968.

Smith, John W., and Bette M. Smith, "Desegregation in the South and the De-mise of the Black Educator," Vol. 20, No. 1, *Journal of the Association of Social and Behavioral Sciences*, 1974.

Smith, Page. *Killing the Spirit; Higher Education in America* (New York: Penguin, 1990).

Stamps, Spurgeon M., and James C. Renick, "Leadership Styles of the Black College President: An Area in Need of Elaboration," Interdisciplinary Social Sci-ences, University of South Florida. No date given.

Stonequist, Everett V. *The Marginal Man* (New York: Scribner's Sons, 1937).

Stowe, Harriet Beecher. *Uncle Tom's Cabin* (New York: Dodd, Mead, 1952).

Vold, George B. *Theoretical Criminology, 2nd Ed.* (New York: Oxford University Press, 1979).

Wesley, Charles H. *Collapse of the Confederacy* (Washington, D.C.: Associated Publishers, 1937).

Wesley, Charles H, with Carter G. Woodson. *The Negro in Our History* (Wash-ington, D.C.: Associated Publishers, 1962).

Wesley, Charles H. *The Negro in the Americas* (Washington, D.C.: Associated Publishers, 1940).

Wilson, William Julius. *The Truly Disadvantaged* (Chicago: The University of Chicago press, 1988).

Zack, Naomi, Ed. *American Mixed Race: The Culture of Microdiversity* (Lanham, MD: Rowman & Littlefield, 1995).

About the Author

Gordon D. Morgan received his early sociological training at Arkansas AM&N College (later renamed University of Arkansas at Pine Bluff). After service in the Korean War, he received the MA degree in sociology at the University of Arkansas. He interned at the Federal Correctional Institution, outside Denver, Colorado. After teaching social science and mathematics at the high school level, in Conway, Arkansas, he took up a position at Arkansas AM&N College. Between assignments he studied at the University of Minnesota. Later he enrolled at Washington State University where he received the Ph.D. degree in 1963. Under the auspices of Teachers College, Columbia University, he served as research assistant in East Africa, where he researched and studied African education and society.

Following that experience, he joined the two-person sociology department at Lincoln University, Jefferson City Missouri, where he worked closely with Oliver C. Cox. In 1969, he joined the sociology department at the University of Arkansas, Fayetteville. During that time he has written some nine published books on many phases of the black and African experience. He has specialized also in the writing of biographies. Among these are: *Lawrence A. Davis: Arkansas Educator* (New York: Associated Faculty Press, 1985); *Ida Rowland Bellegarde: Master Teacher/Scholar* (New York: McGraw-Hill, 1992); *Tilman C. Cothran: Second Generation Sociologist* (Bristol, IN: Wyndham Hall Press, 1994).

Among his other works is listed *America Without Ethnicity* (Port Washington, New York: Kennikat, 1981 and, with Izola Preston, *The Edge of Campus: An Informal History of the Black Experience at the University of Arkansas* (Fayetteville: University of Arkansas Press, 1990).

Mr. Morgan has held post-doctoral fellowships from the American College Testing Program, and the Ford Foundation resulting in *The Ghetto College Student, 1970.* A Russell Sage Foundation post-doctoral resulted in "Black Hillbillies of the Arkansas Ozarks," 1972.

He has served as Distinguished Visiting Professor at Washington State University. His latest work is entitled *Toward an American Sociology: Questioning the European Construct* (Westport, CT: Praeger, 1997).

He is currently engaged in writings and studies of whiteness while serving as University Professor at the University of Arkansas.

Index

www.ingramcontent.com/pod-product-compliance
Lightning Source LLC
Chambersburg PA
CBHW021158010426
R18062100001B/R180621PG41931CBX00020B/35